Richard III

i

IAN McKELLEN

WILLIAM SHAKESPEARE'S
RICHARD III

A SCREENPLAY WRITTEN BY
IAN McKELLEN & RICHARD LONCRAINE,
ANNOTATED & INTRODUCED BY IAN McKELLEN

Doubleday

LONDON · NEW YORK · TORONTO · SYDNEY · AUCKLAND

TRANSWORLD PUBLISHERS LTD
61-63 Uxbridge Road, London W5 5SA

TRANSWORLD PUBLISHERS (AUSTRALIA) PTY LTD
15-25 Helles Avenue, Moorebank, NSW 2170

TRANSWORLD PUBLISHERS (NZ) LTD
3 William Pickering Drive, Albany, Auckland

Published 1996 by Doubleday
a division of Transworld Publishers Ltd

A catalogue record for this book is available
from the British Library.

ISBN 0 385 40801 3

Set in Monotype Bembo
by Phoenix Typesetting, Ilkley, West Yorkshire

Printed in Great Britain
by Mackays of Chatham plc, Chatham, Kent

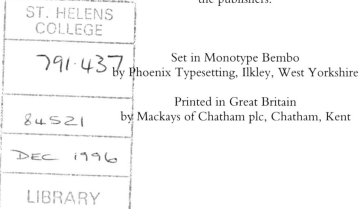

For Pieter Rogers
without whose suggestion
I should never have played Richard III.

INTRODUCTION

'If you really want to play Richard III on film, you'd better write the screenplay.' Richard Eyre, director of the Royal National Theatre of Great Britain (RNT), spoke this as a warning but with a twinkle in his eye, knowing that I would be foolhardy enough to pick up the challenge. Eighteen months earlier, his production of *Richard III* had opened at the RNT's Lyttelton Theatre in London and then toured the United Kingdom. We had crossed Europe, from west to east, en route to Cairo and Tokyo. After 150 performances, I was reluctant to let go of our success and so, with some cast changes, we revived the show and continued, till we found ourselves in New York on 1 June 1992, starting a fifteen-week tour of the United States. The production would finally close in Los Angeles.

When the run ends, a theatre production survives only in the fading memories of those who were there in person – in the audience, onstage or backstage. Previous Richard IIIs, like David Garrick and Henry Irving, even my contemporaries like Al Pacino and Tony Sher, still trail glory but, despite prints and photographs, memoirs and memorabilia, their success is no longer tangible. Yet Laurence Olivier triumphantly transferred his *Richard III* from stage to screen.

The most obvious way of preserving a live performance is the least satisfactory. Our *Richard III* had already been fixed for posterity on 26 May 1992, when three cameras were let into the Lyttelton Theatre, as part of the British Theatre Museum's experiment in saving plays for the future, by recording them during a scheduled public performance. It was agreed that the three separate video-tapes would never be edited and could only ever be viewed simultaneously by a visitor to the Museum in Covent Garden. The adjacent screens show the full stage, the principals in each scene, and a close-up of whoever is speaking, so that the viewer, rather like a theatre audience, can 'edit' the production, by switching attention between the three images. This triple record may be adequate for academic study, visually augmenting the stage-manager's prompt-book that tabulates the actors' moves. It does not, unfortunately, capture much of the impact of the original occasion.

Innumerable Shakespeare stage productions have been more subtly photographed and then edited for network television. I've been in four of these. In 1969, having played Shakespeare's *Richard II* on tour and in London, the actors of Prospect Theatre were invited by BBC TV to reproduce our performance, as best we could, for their video cameras, within the simplest of studio settings. Viewing the result twenty-five years on, I am embarrassed. The interpretation of the play by the director, Richard Cottrell, and by his cast withstands time well enough and, maybe, outclasses subsequent productions in intelligence and insight. It is, however, very poor television. My own performance is accurately recorded but so too is a theatricality that bombasts the viewers, in my determination to excite and enthral them.

It was much the same with my *Hamlet* two years later, which Robert Chetwyn directed, again for Prospect Theatre. The televised version now looks less like a play and more like a dramatised commentary running alongside the action – interesting enough for students of the text but not credible for anyone hoping to meet Hamlet rather than Ian-McKellen-playing-Hamlet. In 1978, when we came to televise the Royal Shakespeare Company's (RSC's) studio version of *Macbeth*, there was the possibility of improvement.

This chamber production had been devised for The Other Place, the now-demolished tin hut, in the car park along from the RSC's main theatre on the banks of the River Avon. The director was Trevor Nunn; the designer was John Napier. Years before their joint talents spectacularly exploded on world theatre with *Cats*, *Les Miserables* and *Sunset Boulevard*, they placed a cast of twelve actors within a magic circle painted on the plain wooden floor. We had no scenery and no changes of costume, except for those who played more than one part. The entire design budget was £200. The visual impact lay in Shakespeare's poetic imagery and nothing interposed between the actors and the audience of a hundred, who crowded around us on three sides of the acting-area. The effect was properly alarming. One priest queued for a returned ticket again and again, so that he could sit at our feet, discreetly holding out his crucifix to protect us from the evil summoned up in the stifling air of The Other Place. Could we ever re-create that atmosphere for the home-viewer?

Trevor Nunn hoped so, saying: 'We will photograph the text.' In a small Granada Television studio in London, he re-arranged our stage moves to accommodate the one camera, whose video-tape was later edited as if it had been film. The air was filled with smoke from oil-canisters and the smoke was lit to indicate the cold of the Scottish heathland or the richness of a castle's interior. There were many close-ups. The limited vocal projection required of the actors for The Other Place was easily adapted for the camera. We retained the same text we had used onstage, which ran for two hours without an interval. Nearly twenty years later, as the story tautly unfolds on the small screen, there is an intimate horror that is still thrilling. The words are paramount and contradict the assumption that television is primarily a visual medium. Within the confines of a small-screen recording of a stage performance, Nunn's *Macbeth* has not been surpassed, even by his own video *Othello*, when I played Iago to Willard White's Moor.

During the day and late into the night after each evening's performance in Washington DC, Minneapolis, Denver and San Francisco, I scribbled long-hand into my foolscap notebook: *Richard III – The Film*. Whether it would be a film for television or for the cinema, I didn't know. Either way, the principle was probably the same – to choose from the play what was most important in terms of plot and interesting in terms of writing and direct the camera's attention so that nothing was missed: then to imagine what pictures and scenery would enhance it all. If, in the process, the play was opened out beyond the confines of what is practical in the theatre, I was only building on the knowledge I had gathered over months of preparation and playing.

Having the finished production so close to hand was a huge advantage: but I was also helped by recalling the preliminary discussions that Richard Eyre and I had with Bob Crowley, the designer, long before we started rehearsals. The three of us had met at least once a week over a couple of months in Richard's office, reading the play outloud together and dissecting it scene by scene. As so often happens with a classic play, we talked about it in the near-present tense and imagined it taking place yesterday rather than yesteryear. This, I suppose, was what Shakespeare intended. The historical events which he used and adapted for his plays were staged as drama not as a history lesson. That is the riposte to those admirers of the real King Richard who complain that Shakespeare's fiction is a slanderous slight on their hero.

The real Richard, Duke of Gloucester, was crowned King of England in 1483, when he was thirty-one years old – that much is certain. The truth about his personality and the circumstances in which he took over the throne continue to be a puzzle to this day.

During the civil wars that divided the country in the middle of the fifteenth century, Richard supported his elder brother Edward's claim to the crown. He remained loyal throughout the reign of the victorious King Edward IV. On Edward's death, his thirteen-year-old son and heir was named King Edward V, with Uncle Richard put in charge of running the country as Lord Protector. Yet within two months, the young king, along with his nine-year-old brother, had disappeared. Rumour said that they were kept within the stone walls of the ancient Tower of London – where state prisoners were incarcerated and executed. It was soon believed that the two lads had been put to death in The Tower, on the direct orders of their uncle, who then reigned as King Richard III. Two years later, Henry Richmond led a rebellion and, at the Battle of Bosworth, Richard III was killed. Richmond was crowned King Henry VII, the first of the Tudor family of monarchs who then governed for more than a century.

So England's turbulent history rolled on. During Henry VII's reign, his official historians elaborated on the gossip about the late Richard III and the doomed Princes in The Tower, substantiating the story of a wicked tyrant who deserved to be deposed by the stalwart Tudor who succeeded him. It has been tellingly pointed out, with regard to the princes' legitimacy to the throne, that Henry VII had just as much to gain as Richard III, by their removal. Richard III's efficiency as a royal administrator was forgotten, along with his military successes in defence of the realm. His faults were stressed and perhaps exaggerated. Even his physical appearance was distorted by time. The real Richard III may have been disabled by a twisted spine but, fifty years after his death, he was described by the historian Edward Hall as 'little of stature, evil-featured of limbs, crook-backed, the left shoulder much higher than the right, hard-favoured of visage. He was malicious, wrathful and envious and it is reported that he came into the world feet forward.' When such details were repeated by Sir Thomas More in his authoritative *History of King Richard III*, the damage to reputation was almost complete. Vilification had been authenticated into history.

Of late, investigators have tried to prove that the real Richard was not after all the child murderer of popular history and that the two princes had survived and even escaped to live out their natural lives with adopted identities. One recent theory is more fascinating than the rest. It claims that the younger prince, the Duke of York, grew up under an assumed name surviving into his early nineties. If that were true, he would have died just as the genius was born who was to transform rumour and history into drama and myth.

The play is not a documentary about the man on whose life it is based. If Shakespeare accepted the Tudor version of the hunchback monster, he nevertheless called his version *The Tragedy of Richard III* (cf. *The Life of Henry V* or *The Famous History of the Life of King Henry VIII*). To direct the audience away from history and toward the events and themes of the play as far as they were relevant to their own lives, the original production would have been performed in contemporary, Elizabethan dress. Historical 'authenticity' of costume and setting only became fashionable in the theatre of the Victorians, with their interest in things medieval.

As with *Hamlet*, *Macbeth*, *Coriolanus*, *Twelfth Night*, *Othello* and all the other Shakespeare I've most enjoyed doing, Richard Eyre's *Richard III* would be staged in a modern context. The clinching moment was when one of us asked: 'How should the Prince of Wales be brought back to London before being sent to The Tower?' One of us said: 'Don't the royals always arrive in London by rail?' And thereafter Act 3 Scene 1 was known as 'Victoria Station'.

The Crowley style of setting was minimal. Victoria Station was conjured up by a red carpet unrolled across the black floor of the empty stage, with a puff of smoke blown in from the wings, as the young Prince of Wales entered to inspect his guard of honour — four actors in red coats and black boots. The architecture, the steam-train and carriages were left to the audience's imagination, aided by the actors' belief in their non-existent surroundings. In my screenplay, all I had to do was fill this out into the setting as described in scene 62.

The crucial advantage of a modern setting is clarity of storytelling. It is impossibly confusing to try and distinguish between a multitude of characters who are all done up in floppy hats and wrinkled tights. *Richard III* has a long, complex cast-list but it is not a pageant. It analyses a sophisticated group of powerful and would-be powerful players. The political detail of the story cannot clearly unfold, unless each of these characters can be readily identified by profession and social status. The audience needs to be able to recognise who is royalty, aristocrat, commoner and who is politician, civil servant, military. By their clothes, you shall know them. If this were true of the play, it would be equally valid for the film.

Onstage it is possible to use an eclectic variety of costuming which does not fix the production in a specific year or century even. That seemed to have no advantage for this play. Nor could we expect our audience to imagine *Richard III* happening in present-day England: that would have only parodied current affairs.

The historical events of the play had occurred just a couple of generations before the first audience saw them dramatised. The comparable period for us would be the 1930s, close enough for no-one to think we were identifying the plot of the play with actual events, any more than Shakespeare was writing about the real King Richard. He was creating history-which-never-happened. Our production was properly in the realm of 'what might have been'. Also, the 30s were appropriately a decade of tyranny throughout Europe, the most recent time when a dictatorship like Richard III's might have overtaken the United Kingdom, as it had done Germany, Italy, Spain and the empire of the Soviet Union.

Audiences across the world took the point and revealed a paradox: the more specific a production, the more general its relevance. Although our story was obviously an English one, audiences took the message personally wherever we toured. In Hamburg, Richard's blackshirt troops seemed like a commentary on the Third Reich. In Bucharest, when Richard was slain, the Romanians stopped the show with heartfelt cheers, in memory of their recent freedom from Ceaucescu's regime. In Cairo, as the Gulf War was hotting up, it all seemed like a new play about Saddam Hussein. One critic lambasted me for poor taste when I ruffled the young prince's hair, before imprisoning him, as Hussein had just been seen doing to a little English boy he had taken hostage. My stage business, of course, had been devised six months previously – life was imitating art. It was reminiscent of the scene in *Arturo Ui*, where Bertholt Brecht's seedy greengrocer learns the art of dictatorship by studying *Richard III* with a ham actor.

The sense of period in Bob Crowley's designs had depended mostly on his costumes and furniture. Scenic effects were created by Jean Kalman's lighting rather than by expressions of architecture. There were no walls, staircases or doors. As with 'Victoria Station', other scenes of the stage production that had been imagined in dining-rooms, committee-rooms, throne-rooms were easy to transcribe to reality. I described in the screenplay what had been my imaginary surroundings onstage and made them specific. I assumed that we should film in the real Tower of London – and I began to look forward to acting close to where the princes had been murdered 500 years ago. The royals in the film would live in Buckingham Palace or more likely its cinematic double, Blenheim Palace. It would be fun filming the politicians in the corridors of The Houses of Parliament and outside 10, Downing Street. Then I went too far.

In Act 3 Scene 2, Catesby the royal courtier calls on the politician Hastings. So I wrote:

26   INT. CATESBY'S OFFICE

Sir William Catesby, the King's private secretary, is on the phone to Lord Hastings, the Prime Minister.

CATESBY

The King's physicians fear him mightily.
Prime Minister, the King doth call for you.

27   INT. HASTINGS' PRIVATE APARTMENT AT 10, DOWNING STREET

Hastings, 60 years old, is answering the phone, as his teenage mistress massages his fat body toward orgasm.

HASTINGS

Catesby, I come!

With this and other infelicities in place, I completed my first draft of my first screenplay just as *Richard III* opened in Los Angeles.

Richard Eyre didn't approve of the modern props which had invaded the storytelling, particularly the telephones, motor cars and battle machinery. He also pointed out that I had written something that no television company could afford to finance these days. 500 costumed extras at a state banquet, for instance, with as many in the battle scenes, plus two dozen grandiose locations across London – such ambitions could only be realised, if at all, by a multi-million-dollar budget. That meant a major movie that would only be able to recover its investment by appealing to a large international audience. Nothing wrong with that, we agreed, except for two things.

The time needed in pre-production for such an enterprise now meant that Richard, with his daily commitments to the RNT, could not be the director. Nor could his original cast expect to retain their parts in a movie directed by someone else. As filmstars dropped by in my dressing-room after the show in Los Angeles, I sized them up. Might Danny De Vito want to play Buckingham? Surely he would prefer Richard III. Patrick Stewart – could Captain Picard be convincing as Clarence? I told Meryl Streep that the film Queen Elizabeth would be played as an American heiress who had married into the British Royal Family. I asked her whether she could do an American accent.

Mixing words and pictures, the screen has its own language. So, in adapting *Richard III* I was translating. Translation is an inexact art, carrying responsibilities to respect the author's ends, even as you wilfully tamper with the means. I hadn't asked for Shakespeare's permission to fashion a film from his play. The least I could do was, change by change, cut by cut, ask myself whether he would have approved. I am used to this discipline. In rehearsing Shakespeare, I puzzle over the complexities of his verse and prose, its ambiguities and subtleties. Not having him present to consult, I think of his having just left the rehearsal-room, soon to return with the gentle query I've sometimes heard from living playwrights: 'What the hell do you think you're doing to my play?' There is always the justification that despite one's amendments, the 'full text' will remain intact in any Collected Plays for the next fool to try and measure up to.

The most obvious difference between a cinema or television version of Shakespeare is in the number of words retained from the original play. A three-hour video can leave most of the text intact and still sell. Most cinema-owners want shorter movies, that get more showings per day. It is not just a matter of time. *Romeo and Juliet*, in modern productions, is a very long play: yet its Chorus refers to 'the two hours' traffic of our stage' (the length, not co-incidentally, of our finished film). Elizabethan actors, playing in small auditoria, would have spoken more quickly than we do today, in deference to their audience, most of whom were standing. In a two-hour talkie, even talking fast, you might just get through two-thirds of *Richard III*, one of the longest plays Shakespeare wrote. A theatre audience, by definition, ought to listen before it looks. Unlike Shakespeare's groundlings, a cinema audience would not stand for it.

Cutting Shakespeare has been going on for 400 years. The length of the first performances in the Globe Theatre would not only have depended upon speed of delivery. What we take to be 'full texts' seem not always to have been the 'acting texts'. No original play-script in Shakespeare's handwriting has survived him: he did not expect to have his work preserved for posterity by publication. Modern editions are an amalgam from a variety of sources – the original manuscript, before and after it was amended for performance; what his cast may have remembered having acted, when consulted months or years later by the publishers; plus the imaginative accretions of subsequent editors. It is known that, on tour, the playtexts were cut for performance in the Elizabethan provinces. Why not also in the original London production? If then, why not today, in the theatre – and on the screen?

As in Richard Eyre's version, the first draft of the screenplay cut some characters and handed over a few of their lines to other characters. This throws emphasis and clarity onto the main action. If it is thought by those who know the play well that I have gone too far in not explaining, for example, how exactly Richard persuades King Edward to imprison their brother Clarence, I am not sure that Shakespeare did much better in what I excised from Act 1 Scene 1! I also cut all mention of Clarence's family and re-imagined him as a bachelor. Too many other children in the film distract from the young princes and their fate in The Tower. The centre of Clarence's impact on the story is his own imprisonment and his nightmare which prefigures other dreams. Similarly, I removed Queen Elizabeth's grown-up children by her first marriage.

The Scrivener (3.6) and other unnamed citizens lost their brief appearances. Although I was reluctant to cut any of the few references to the world outside the corridors of power, it was possible to compensate visually with glimpses of the hospital in scene 23 and the political rally in scene 87.

I combed through the entire text to shorten it but without losing any of the detailed development of plot or character. Some reduction of the play's verbal impact was inevitable but much less damaging than in, say, *Macbeth*, where every poetical line is interdependent on the rest. The verse and language of *Richard III*, a much earlier play, are less dense than in the great tragedies. Although the young Shakespeare was writing almost entirely in verse, he frequently captured a conversational tone, which some recent stage Richards (or at least their directors) have missed. It is a tone that is ideal for the cinema.

The text I decided on in the first draft was changed very little by subsequent versions but one cut, draft by draft, I resisted. The widowed Queen Margaret represents the Lancastrian dynasty which Richard overthrew by killing her husband. She haunts *Richard III* like a living ghost, referring back to the recent and distant past. Yet, even theatre audiences are confused by her persistent litany of revenge. In the film, her powerful presence would not compensate for the time spent in explaining clearly who she is and has been. Once removed, Queen Margaret as a symbol of the past was replaced, in part, by the matriarchal Duchess of York, who took over a few of her lines. In doing this, there was a change in emphasis. If the action of the play often looks back, the film is centred on the living moment and then looks forward. That impetus was underlined by bringing to life Princess Elizabeth, who in the play is an offstage character, even though she ends up as Queen of England. I similarly expanded the presence of Richmond, her husband-to-be.

Richard Gloucester's famous opening monologue recalls a civil war just ended, in which he had been an active participant. Shakespeare had already written three five-act plays about the Wars of the

Roses. *Henry VI parts 1, 2 and 3* lengthily explore the dynastic relationships through three generations, whose ambitions, betrayals and murders inform the vengeful resolution in *Richard III*. These historical events were recent enough to have been familiar to Shakespeare's original audience: but 400 years on, we need help.

Of late, in the United Kingdom, theatre companies have followed the example of Peter Hall's *Wars of the Roses* (RSC, 1963) by presenting cut-down versions of all four plays played over two or three evenings. This is an ambitious solution to the exposition problem! Once they have endured six-or-more hours of the complications of the *Henry VI* trio, audiences reach the relatively simple progress of *Richard III*'s plottings with relief – and with self-congratulation that, by that time, they can confidently identify all the characters and tell even a hawk from a handsaw.

Alternatively, the theatre programme for a *Richard III* on its own can tabulate royal family-trees and copious biographies: but it is difficult to study English history in the gloom of an auditorium. One production I saw boldly marched all the characters onstage before the play began and introduced them by name. The audience's panic was palpable, as they failed to grasp what was going on, let alone who was who.

Richard Eyre's production had the legend 'Edward IV' projected onto the front curtain, confusing some to think they had arrived at the wrong play! Behind it I was waiting. Then there was a black-out, the scream of a horse in agony and the startling clang and clash of armaments, overwhelmed by shouts of victory. The curtain invisibly rose and the lights came up on the now silent, smoke-filled stage. Richard emerged from the back and slowly limped forward to address his audience. The first of the storytellers had arrived onstage – his colleagues waiting in the wings. The play began.

The place and time were no more defined than 'here and now'. Indeed 'Now' is the first word spoken. In what real 'here and now' should I place Richard – the reality, that is, of the screen?

A familiar cinematic solution is a caption indicating 'the story so far' but I was initially reluctant to pre-empt Shakespeare's opening words with some of my own. Shouldn't the film start with pictures

rather than words? Shouldn't we actually see Richard killing King Henry VI and his son the Prince of Wales, both of whose widows survive as part of the continuing story? So I recapitulated.
First draft: October 1992 –

A black screen:

> CAPTION – LONDON, ENGLAND: 1934

> A number of pistol shots illuminate the prone KING HENRY VI.

> A silver lighter lights a cigarette and is held out, as a hand checks the pulse of the new corpse. On the bedside table is a photo of KING HENRY VI and his QUEEN MARGARET. The lighter goes out.

CAPTION:

> THE TRAGEDY of RICHARD III

That got expanded.
Second draft: January 1993 –

> A black screen:
> CAPTION – LONDON, ENGLAND.

> **INT. TOWER OF LONDON PRISON – DEAD OF NIGHT**

> A small cell where old KING HENRY VI is kept in solitary confinement.

Out of the almost total dark, there are ugly sounds of stabbing, struggling and pain, as a murder is invisibly committed. Guilty footsteps retreat as a cell door is opened – an imposing silhouette enters, as the door opens and is smartly closed.

In the foreground, a gunmetal Zippo lighter lights an Abdulla cigarette and reveals, beyond, the prone, butchered, dying KING HENRY VI. The old man stares up, as the same hand, still holding the lighter, dextrously cocks a military revolver, takes expert aim and fires the coup de grâce. The flash is blinding. The KING is dead. Outside, footsteps approach along the flagstones. The lighter clicks out as the door is flung open. The light behind them is enough to see the corpse's aged widow QUEEN MARGARET and his glamorous daughter-in-law LADY ANNE. They are aghast at the bloody mess. LADY ANNE faints but QUEEN MARGARET recognises the figure still holding the revolver. She opens her mouth to scream. Her wailing continues over . . .

CAPTION:

THE TRAGEDY of RICHARD III.

Third draft: January 1994 –

1   **EXT. ROYAL FAMILY VAULT – DAY**

The sun shines on the medieval vault, protected by a barbed-wire enclosure, set in an English parkland that shows the destructive ravages of a prolonged civil war. In the distance, smoke rises from the battlefield.

The ROYAL PARTY slowly approaches, preceded by two GUARDS, carrying three floral wreaths. These are ceremonially handed to KING HENRY VI (black armband on his naval uniform) and his wife QUEEN MARGARET and their daughter-in-law LADY ANNE – both veiled in deep, funereal mourning. A flashbulb flashes. The scene is recorded.

The Royal Party enters the dark interior.

The large, wooden door closes, leaving the guards outside.

2   **INT. ROYAL FAMILY VAULT – DAY**

Dusty sunbeams fall through the stained-glass windows, colouring the stone floor. Pillars, statues, candles.

King Henry VI, Queen Margaret and Lady Anne walk to a new mausoleum. Their FOOTSTEPS ECHO in the silence.

The King and Queen place their tributes against the marble plinth.

Queen Margaret lifts her heavy veil and puts on her glasses/lorgnettes to read the inscription:

'HRH PRINCE EDWARD
SON TO
HM KING HENRY VI & QUEEN MARGARET'

King Henry VI is kneeling in prayer.

Queen Margaret rises to join Lady Anne on the other side of the monument.

Lady Anne, deeply distressed, has placed her wreath under the second inscription:

'HUSBAND TO
LADY ANNE OF WARWICK'

Queen Margaret stoically comforts her daughter-in-law.

From the other side of the tomb, there are oddly sinister sounds of muffled violence and a long gasp for breath.

Queen Margaret, alarmed, moves round to see King Henry VI slumped to the floor, lying in a pool of stained-glass light.

Assassination!

Lady Anne joins her mother-in-law. As she turns over King Henry VI's body, she faints and falls into his pool of blood.

There is a CLICK of a gunmetal Zippo as an Abdulla is lit in this holy place.

Queen Margaret glances up. She mouths his name.

ZOOM IN to see, for the first time, the grim, half-lit face of RICHARD, Duke of Gloucester. He is sweating.

> RICHARD
> (quietly triumphant)
> **Now is the winter of our discontent**
> **Made glorious summer by this son of York!**

Richard points at himself.

CAPTION:

> RICHARD III – a Tragedy by William Shakespeare.

Having settled on a final draft, which was eventually filmed and which can now be read here, the opening lines were further delayed by the Victory Ball scenes, which introduced the principle players.

Before 1990, I had had no interest in playing Richard III. Indeed, I had long dismissed the play as not fit for modern consumption. Its sell-by date had surely expired, once modern psychology had questioned the cruel assumption of Shakespeare's contemporaries that physical deformity was an outward expression of some inner moral turpitude. Studying the play reveals an opposite proposition – that Richard's wickedness is an outcome of other people's disaffection with his physique. His mother's cursing outburst in scene 97 exemplifies the verbal and emotional abuse which from infancy has formed her youngest son's character and behaviour. Academics can be too adamant when exploring the origins of Elizabethan drama. They note the symbolism of characters in those medieval morality plays with which Shakespeare was undoubtedly familiar. They miss what actors discover, that Shakespeare fleshed-out those types and made them human.

It is an odd, critical commonplace that, despite so many performances to the contrary, Richard III is still accepted as an embodiment of pure evil. This charge has also been levelled at Iago. Having just played that part and delved into the jealous psychology of a sexually frustrated husband, I was prepared to explore Richard's humanity rather than reducing him to an emblem of wickedness.

All of Shakespeare's troubled heroes reveal their inner selves in their confidential soliloquies. These are not thoughts-out-loud, rather true confessions to the audience. Richard may lie to all the other characters but within his solo speeches he always tells the truth. I never doubted that in the film he would have to break through the fourth wall of the screen and talk directly to the camera, as to a confidant. If this unsettled the audience, so much the better. They should not be comfortable hearing his vile secrets and being treated as accomplices. They would also better appreciate the brilliance of his ability to fool, deceive and seduce his hapless victims. Men and women are all players to Shakespeare but Richard is a consummate actor.

He is also a professional fighting soldier. Shakespeare, throughout his work, returned to what seems like an obsession with the behaviour of the military during peacetime. *Othello*, *Troilus & Cressida* and *Much Ado About Nothing* deal with troops of soldiers who, idle after battle, make mischief. *Macbeth*, *Coriolanus*, *Julius Caesar* each examine individual charismatic and admirable commanders who, disastrously for themselves and others, blunder into civilian politics. One of the themes of *Richard III* is proven by modern history – that good generals do not necessarily make good statesmen. Some actors have thought to play him as a mass murderer. But he is a tyrant not a psychopath. Indeed, rather late in the day, he reveals a troubled conscience in his final, alarming soliloquy. I attempted to make this guilt more credible in the screenplay, helped by cinematic close-up, by hinting at Richard's inner moral turmoil each time a victim dies. As for the actual killings, I expanded the presence of Tyrell, the play's disaffected gentleman, and made him the subordinate who was prepared to obey any order from his superior officer.

This interpretation is at odds with the tradition of *Richard III* as primarily a star vehicle. Colley Cibber set the pattern in 1700 when he literally made the part his own. He slashed the text and added as many of his own lines to what was left. Since him, the play has attracted a multitude of leading actors and never been out of fashion with theatre-goers all over the world. Then in 1956, cinema audiences were introduced to Laurence Olivier's overwhelming performance. Although he included a couple of Cibber's more famous additions he removed Queen Margaret and most of Queen Elizabeth and the Duchess of York. Of late, in the theatre, the supporting characters have been given more attention, revealing a family drama of power-politics, more tragic than melodramatic. Our film represents that re-assessment of *Richard III* as much more than a one-man show.

Something similar is true of *Henry V*. Olivier's war-time film was immediately popular in 1944, because it stressed the patriotism of an English king vanquishing a foreign power. Each generation has always been able to extract from Shakespeare its own message. On many stages, from the 1960s onwards, as European peace prevailed, directors discovered within *Henry V* an anti-war theme. When Adrian Noble cast the 24-year-old Kenneth Branagh in his Royal Shakespeare Company production in 1984, audiences marvelled at the young actor's assured expertise and a star was born. But there was nothing revolutionary about Noble's view of the play as a sombre exposé of the misery of war. When Branagh transferred his performance to film, cinema audiences and critics who don't go to the theatre were understandably astonished by a *Henry V* which re-interpreted the text they knew only from Olivier's film.

Branagh's success with *Henry V* and *Much Ado About Nothing* and Franco Zeffirelli's *Hamlet* starring Mel Gibson were fresh in the minds of financiers whom I hoped to interest in another film based on a very popular Shakespeare play, which could be screened in mainstream cinemas round the world. To prepare myself I eschewed all offers of theatre work and acted exclusively for the screen in mainly supporting or small parts. By visiting other people's films I gained confidence in front of the cameras.

At the same time, I was steered around the major studios in Hollywood, screenplay in one hand, my agent in the other. If only one of those large self-contained organisations would take over the screenplay, they would also buy all the distribution rights worldwide and off to work we would go. I pointed out with confidence to polite, junior studio-executives that, these days, filmed stage classics need not belong only in art-houses and that this particular story of intrigue and murder could be universally popular. There was a general muted enthusiasm and some promises to consider buying the movie once it was made but with no suggestion of any loan in the meantime. One studio boss read the script and telephoned me to say that *Richard III* was 'too dark: the public only wants Pollyanna Shakespeare'.

I also tackled independent producers who, with little money of their own, raise financial backing for films by selling piecemeal the rights to show them in separate territories round the world. In London, one of these bought me lunch and took away the script, since when I have heard nothing from him, except by hearsay: 'Ian McKellen will never get that film going.'

Anyway he was too late, because in Los Angeles my agent David Saunders of A.P.A. had discovered allies at First Look Pictures. This husband-and-wife team, Ellen and Robby Little, needed no persuasion and bought the rights to the second draft of the screenplay. Robby and I were born within fifty miles of each other in the north of England and Ellen met him when she was a student of Renaissance art: kindred spirits. Crucially, they were unfazed by the idea of a middle-aged, English stage-actor hoping to star in an international movie! So, off we went to the 1993 Cannes Film Festival, to look for investors.

I was a fool to think we were home and dry. It is a laborious process convincing cinema-owners in disparate countries that their audiences will eventually enjoy a film when it is still nothing more than words and dreams in a screenplay. As the Littles talked to the Japanese, the Spanish and the Italians, I could see their problem. Thus far, all they had to sell was their own enthusiasm for Shakespeare and for me. A large percentage of audiences for an English-language movie see it with subtitles or dubbed into their own language. So much for the selling power of Shakespeare's verse. Of course, if Ken or Mel or, best of all Arnie or Sly were cast as Richard, it would have been easier. Some promises of money slowly dribbled in from a world I knew nothing of – banks, investors and cinema conglomerates. I couldn't be much help to the Littles. Eighteen months later, the promises had dried up, when Lisa Katselas Paré and her partner Steven Bayly amicably took over as the full-time producers.

They were well-suited to the daunting job of instilling confidence in potential investors. As Americans working in London, they could plausibly present the case for an English-based project which would be aimed at an international audience. Once they had interested United Artists in acquiring the rights to distribution in North America, the film acquired a status elsewhere. North America is universally known as 'domestic', wherever a film is to be made. 'Foreign' means simply 'anywhere other than USA' including the United Kingdom. Any fear I had that therefore Hollywood might patronisingly think of *Richard III* as a minor foreign venture was dispelled once I met the urbane anglophile John Calley, studio head of United Artists, and his colleague James Middleton. They realised the obvious – that there has always been a large audience for Shakespeare and that our film might have a long shelf-life on video. Calley also had a hunch that if the finished film were as accessible as the screenplay, there was a chance that it might also draw an audience for whom 'Shakespeare' has previously spelled boredom and incomprehension. His foresight gave confidence to other distributors. In London, Ian Scorer and Zakiya Powell of Mayfair Entertainment International made their bid to distribute the film beyond the 'domestic' territory.

Nothing that followed on from this strong support by Paré, Bayly, MGM/UA and Mayfair and British Screen Ltd and BSkyB would have been possible without Richard Loncraine, the director. Unknowingly, I had admired his work for years; his films, of course, but also his 400 or so anonymous commercials and the executive toys, including 'Newton's Cradle' which he developed and marketed so successfully. Richard likes to know how everything works: his house is full of bicycles, cameras and computers, all in immaculately working order. Every detail of film-making fascinates him, from the practical mechanics and the artistic considerations of design and casting, through to marketing. Had I known this at our first meeting, I should have been even more grateful than I was that he really liked my screenplay and wanted to bring it to the screen. Yet when he came round to talk, he stressed his reticence.

Like many film professionals, he rarely goes to the theatre and is impervious to its allure. Consequently, his view of Shakespeare has not developed beyond the distorted perspective of stage productions remembered from his youth. That is why he found the directness of the screenplay so appealing. He did not take on the job with a missionary zeal but simply as a director who recognised a gripping story that he could make work excitingly on screen. We were ideally matched, ready to defer to each other's expertise and to learn. We began with a rigorous re-look at the screenplay. From now on I'll call him RL.

I was prepared for the worst – that RL might want me to go back and start all over. He didn't. The text entranced him enough scene by scene that his suggestions were all to do with pictures rather than words, with the style of presentation and of filming. As he described his visual responses, my job as his co-writer became clear. I had to make sure that Shakespeare did not become overwhelmed and that, however it was decorated, the film would remain rooted in his words and his intentions as I understood them. The notes which follow clarify the origins of the film in Shakespeare's text and in Richard Eyre's production of it, however distant those may now be. Our final screenplay follows my first draft, in that the spoken text remains almost as I had cut it two years previously.

I turned down all work that would compete for my time, so that for three months, almost each day, we could re-work the screenplay, usually at RL's house, sustained by the cooking and encouragement of Felice Loncraine. She too is a screenplay writer. Our plan was simple – together we imagined what we wanted, then I went home to put it on the page for others to read. Between times, we communicated by fax and by telephone. RL tried to explain the miracles of the modem so that our word processors might mate in the ether: but he failed. Now, a year since we started, it is difficult to be certain which ideas came from me and which from him. The happy truth is that we did it together.

One immediate decision was made: we would not, as I had planned, set the film within familiar public buildings in London. If our story was a piece of fictitious history, I agreed that easily recognisable locations should be avoided. The Tower of London was re-labelled 'The Tower' and Buckingham Palace became simply 'The Royal Palace'. The art department would scout for photogenic buildings more appropriate than famous tourist sites which carry with them irrelevant connotations.

Our imaginations were not always allowed to run free. Although I was kept in touch with the ups-and-downs and the ins-and-outs of the money-raising, these were not my responsibility. I could not, though, be sheltered from them, whenever they trespassed onto artistic considerations. A budget was set, based on what the distributors guessed they might get back from ticket sales. About £6,000,000 seemed to be the limit; a low budget for such a visually ambitious movie. Our locations would have to be within striking distance of London, to cut down on heavy travel and accommodation costs. There were casting implications too. Our distributors were adamant that two or three of the actors should be internationally famous, yet we could not afford their usual salaries and allowances. We would be dependent on the goodwill of all the cast, crew and technicians to whom we could offer only minimum wages. Those who are credited at the end of this book are generous adventurers, to whom I shall always be grateful.

I began to meet these recruits to our enterprise, often at Shepperton Studios where our central office masterminded the schedule over nine weeks of pre-production. At his Shepperton workshop, I met Daniel Parker, fresh from his Oscar nomination for his work on the monster in *Mary Shelley's Frankenstein*. He would design my make-up.

There are many graphic descriptions of Richard's appearance in
Henry VI Part 3. In *Richard III*, there is scope for the actor to
identify his own deformity. I had shown RL the following extracts
(**heavy type** denotes what was included in the screenplay).

I that am not shaped for sportive tricks,
Nor made to court an amorous looking-glass;
I that am rudely-stamped . . .
I that am curtailed of this fair proportion,
Cheated of feature by dissembling nature,
Deformed, unfinished . . . scarce half made up
And that so lamely and unfashionable
That dogs bark at me as I pass by them. (Richard)

my own deformity . . . me that halts and am mis-shapen
thus (Richard)

Behold my arm is like a blasted sapling withered up
(Richard)

thou lump of foul deformity . . . diffused infection of a man . . .
hedgehog . . . a fouler toad . . . (Lady Anne)

that bottled spider (Queen Elizabeth)

That foul bunch-backed toad
that deadly eye of yours . . . Thou elvish-marked, abortive,
rooting hog . . . (Margaret)

Thou toad (Duchess of York)

There have been Richards who took their enemies' insults at face
value and modelled their make-up and gait on spiders and on toads.
I wanted to look like a soldier who has conquered his incapacities
and, as onstage, base my appearance on Richard's first honest
reference to his deformity as being 'half made-up'. That clue led to

Richard's 'good side' (the right) and his 'bad side' (the left). So I limped on my left leg and kept my useless left arm out of sight except in scene 71. The left side of my face would hang somewhat, congenitally struck.

Daniel Parker moulded three gelatinous, sagging shapes which were glued under my left eye and left jaw to exaggerate my bags and jowl, with the third appearing to pull down my upper lip – again on the left side. This last was soon replaced by a sturdier moulding of latex that would not melt as hot liquids and food passed it by at lunch breaks. The mouth was further distorted by a lower-set of stained teeth. The left eye carried a hand-painted contact lens, reducing the size of my pupil but as this registered only when the camera was close, I was spared its discomfort most of the time. Thanks to the part-inherited expertise of Daniel (his father was the famous make-up man Charlie Parker) none of these additions looked false nor impeded my facial or vocal expression.

Each day's shooting began in Daniel's private make-up van two and a half hours before I was needed on set to film. Often I snoozed, but most of the time I enjoyed watching a master at work, as he coloured over the prosthetics with a variety of paints and greases. Before he stuck on Richard's pencil-line moustache (my idea), I visited the main make-up trailer for my shortcut hair to be greased and combed back into a flat 30s style by Stephen Rose. The third of my daily friends who helped soothe my early-morning grumps was my colleague from the theatre, Mig Kimpton, who produced my solo show *Acting Shakespeare* on its tour of the United Kingdom six years ago. He was keen to see a film being made at close-quarters. In exchange, he gave me constant company and help each day. Mig completed Richard's appearance by slipping the latex hump into its pocket below my left shoulder. My spine twisted along with the rest, looking in the mirror in my caravan, I could believe myself to be 'rudely-stamped' ready to limp out and onto the set.

During the week's rehearsal in Cecil Sharpe House in Regent's Park, where the cast met to read the text and talk about their characters' relationships, I realised that I was no longer looking back to the stage production but, like the rest of my colleagues, was absorbed in the requirements of film and was testing the adequacy of our adaptation.

Common to the play and screenplay was the text. The day before rehearsals, I wrote a letter to RL.

> 'I'm glad at last we're going to do this film.
> Three years has been a long, long time to wait.
> But now I thought I should sit down and try
> to clarify what blank verse means to me;
> and thereby re-assure your doubting heart.
> If, incidentally, you read these lines out loud,
> I'm sure you'll find them tripping off the tongue.
> And yet, of course, they're written in blank verse!
>
> I'll stop that game and go back to the start.
> (And that's another blank verse line, dear heart!)

Before Christopher Marlowe (who was born in 1564, the same year as Shakespeare) came down from Cambridge and wrote his first play, the only English drama had been written in rather doggerely verse and told simple allegorical stories about good and evil, mostly culled from the Bible. Marlowe was also concerned with morality but introduced to the London stage fictional stories about famous people (Tamburlaine the Great and Dr Faustus, for example). He needed a more pliant sort of speech than the old drama. It didn't occcur to him that the prose of everyday speech would be appropriate – after all, his characters were often bigger than life and he wanted them to sound especially grand. And so he lighted upon a formal rhythm which linked all the possibilities of poetry with the informality of the audience's normal speech.

Blank verse means verse that doesn't rhyme. Its meter is called pentameter because there are five (the Greek 'penta') feet to each line. Each foot contains two beats, in the rhythm of the heart – 'de-*dum*' – with the stress on the second beat. And that's all there is to it. I like the heartbeat point – just as it's nice that we have ten fingers and that the blank verse line has ten beats. I imagine Marlowe counting out the beat with his digits. Not that he'd really have needed to, because (cf. my opening paragraph) the general rhythm of English speech – even modern English – often coincides with the sound of blank verse.

Shakespeare took blank verse and ran with it. By the end of his career – in *The Winter's Tale*, say, or *Anthony & Cleopatra* – he scarcely wrote a regular blank verse line, being more fascinated by complicated counterpoint and jazzy rhythms. But *Richard III* is an early play – the first really good one he wrote. He was still intrigued by how easy it is to fall into the rhythm of 'De-*dum*, de-*dum*, de-*dum*, de-*dum*, de-*dum*' and also how fitting it is for whenever the character should sound either rhetorical–

e.g. Lady Anne:

O, curséd be the hand that made these holes;
Curséd the heart that had the heart to do it;
Curséd the blood that let this blood from
hence . . .

or, Lady Anne again, perfectly ordinary–

I will not be your executioner.

Once we accept that a distinguishing mark of our screenplay is a lot of words, that we are making a talky talkie, then I don't think the particular way the words are spread out on the page is an obstacle. Shakespeare made no attempt to have his plays printed and would only want his words to be judged by how they sounded not what they looked like. That's why academic critics get it wrong when they talk about 'verse-speaking', as if somehow it were different from prose-speaking. It never worries me – in fact I'm *delighted* – if the audience never realises that the play is written in verse. The only time when they need to realise it is when the verse rhymes – usually to mark the conclusion of a long scene–

Shine out fair sun, till I have bought a glass,
That I may see my shadow as I pass.

So I don't think there are any hard and fast rules about speaking Shakespeare. But I do think that it's worth the actors examining the verse, to discover how it can help them. Some of the words are old fashioned – that's why I've cut out all the 'thees' and 'thous'. Some other words are unusual and some specially invented – but I promise you that Zeffirelli's *Hamlet* and Branagh's *Much Ado* had *many* more archaisms than are in our script.

I hope you'll want you and me to go through it all line by line but here are a few general notes that I would expect the cast to take into account, as they indicate that the verse is designed to help and not hinder:

1 Read the line out loud and over-stress the 'de-*dum*'s – e.g. Clarence:

'No, *no*, my *dream* was *length*ened *aft*-er *life*'
De-*dum* de-*dum* de-*dum* de-*dum* de-*dum*

That suggests, for instance, that the second 'no' should be spoken with more stress than the first, giving an impetus to the urgency with which Clarence goes on to explain what he felt next. An actor inexperienced in blank verse might (wrongly?) be tempted to think the second 'no' was a bit of over-writing and throw it away. In other words, Shakespeare's rhythm can suggest just how he wants the lines to be spoken.

2 Appreciate that the last word of the line is invariably the most important for the sense and for the sound and it is a sort of teaser, leading on to the beginning of the line that

follows. That's the energy of blank verse – it is always moving onwards, often urgently.

It's intriguing how the last words (which will include the final '*dum*') of the lines in a long speech invariably carry the meaning of the whole. Take Clarence's speech in jail in scene 36:

> **O, I have passed a miserable** night.
> **I thought that I had broken from the** Tower
> **And was embarked to cross to** Burgundy:
> **And in my company my brother** Richard,
> **Who from my cabin tempted me to** walk
> **Upon the hatches. As we paced** along,
> **I thought that Richard struck** me
> **Into the tumbling billows of the** main.
> **O Lord, I thought what pain it was to** drown!
> **What dreadful noise of water in my** ears!
> **What ugly sights of death within my** eyes!
> **I thought I saw a thousand fearful** wrecks,
> **A thousand men that fishes gnawed** upon,
> **Wedges of cold, great anchors, heaps of** pearl,
> **Inestimable stones, unvalued** jewels
> **All scattered in the bottom of the** sea.

In comparison, the *first* syllable (an unstressed 'de') is relatively unimportant.

3 In regular blank verse, each line generally contains one thought, so that the speeches are made up of a series of logical links. It disturbs this forward movement if the actor does too many 'naturalistic' pauses in the middle of the lines. Shakespeare's characters love talking but not necessarily the sound of their own voices. Speech and thought are simultaneous. The time for the actors to think what they will say next is whilst someone else is speaking. During their own speeches, the natural place to pause (but then only when really necessary for effect) is usually at

the end of the blank verse line – even if the end of a
sentence occurs in the middle of the line. e.g. Clarence
again:

And in my company my brother Richard,
Who from my cabin tempted me to walk
Upon the hatches. As we paced along . . .

The sense and sentence finish with 'hatches.' in the
middle of the line. If Clarence pushes on from there, without
more than a breath, with 'As we paced along', he will
capture the character's desperation (a) to tell the story of his
dream while it's still fresh in his memory and (b) to convey
the turbulence with which each succeeding image of the
dream turned it into a nightmare. The arrangement of the
verse indicates to the actor that the speech is not reflective
but urgent.

4 There is never a need for the verse to be obvious to the
   audience. The 'voice beautiful' is a relic not of
   Shakespeare's style but of Victorian theatres, which were
   so huge that actors needed to sing out the lines in order to
   be heard at the back of the distant gallery. I would expect
   our dialogue to sound swiftly conversational most of the
   time; as Hamlet advised the actors at Elsinore:

   Speak the speech, I pray you, as I pronounced it
   to you, trippingly on the tongue. But if you
   'mouth' it, as many of your players do, I had as
   lief the town-crier spoke my lines.

   And that, for now, is all I've got to say.'

The notes which accompany the screenplay are all my own work
and any errors of fact or judgement are all my fault. Whilst I was
writing, RL was still busy on post-production, overseeing the
sound, music and final colour-grading of the film. By a happy

chance I delivered this book to my ever helpful editor Alison Tulett on the same day that post-production on the film was completed – Friday, 17 November 1995.

There were half-a-dozen cinemas in the northern town of Wigan, where I was brought up in the 1940s, that changed their programmes once or twice a week. Most of them were rather grubby and visiting them was not a glamorous outing. The carpets were threadbare, the toilets smelly and the seats rickety. The back row had double-seats, with no arm-rests to divide courting couples from each other's attentions in the dark. We watched the movie screen through the brightly lit haze of cigarette smoke that floated up and along the beam from the projectionist's lantern. Pipes and cigars were not permitted. In the intervals between the trailers and the adverts and again between the Pathé or Movietone Newsreel and the 'B' movie and again between more ads and the Big Feature, watery ice-creams were on sale from the pinafored sales-girls who sauntered up and down the steep aisles, waving their flashlights between the maroon, velvet rows. These were the flea-pits where dreams and fantasies bred among the germs.

My parents didn't go to the pictures very often. As a family we preferred the theatre, whether the local Hippodrome, with its weekly diet of thrillers, comedies and farces or Manchester's Palace and Opera House where meatier fare was served, en route for the West End. Long before I went to Stratford-upon-Avon for the summer festival of Shakespeare, I discovered his plays at the amateur Little Theatres in Wigan and nearby Bolton and in the big touring productions from the Old Vic. Shakespeare has ever since dominated my lifelong passion for the theatre. Knowledge of his plays helped with my entrance examinations for Cambridge University, where some success in undergraduate amateur dramatics suggested that I might be good enough to become a professional actor. I promised my sceptical father that I would give it a go for a couple of years before abandoning acting for teaching or journalism or, more likely, for unemployment.

During the last very fulfilling thirty-five years, my sorties into screen-acting have been few, more by chance than intention. Long-term contracts with Prospect, RSC and RNT have inhibited a career in films. Yet during the three years it has taken to realise the film of *Richard III*, I have often recalled a decisive moment pre-dating any serious ambition to be an actor, let alone a film-actor.

In 1958 I saw Laurence Olivier's *Richard III* at the Odeon Cinema in Bolton. A spell was cast as I watched the shadows of great actors and I had confirmed my juvenile sense that Shakespeare was for everybody. I hope that today's young audience might feel something similar when they see our film.

Ian McKellen,
London E14, November 1995

RICHARD III

SCREENPLAY

The unit photographer plays a vital role by recording each scene as it is shot. The first public images of *Richard III*, before the trailer and film-clips, have been Alex Bailey's evocative stills, 59 of which illustrate this Screenplay.

The Screenplay has 126 scenes. Other numbering (eg. 1.1) refer to the acts and scenes of standard editions of the play.

WHO'S WHO

OLD ROYAL FAMILY
> KING HENRY
> PRINCE EDWARD, his only son
> LADY ANNE, Prince Edward's widow, later married
> to Richard

NEW ROYAL FAMILY
> DUCHESS OF YORK, widow
> KING EDWARD, her eldest son
> QUEEN ELIZABETH, his wife
> PRINCESS ELIZABETH, 15, their daughter
> PRINCE OF WALES, 12, their eldest son and heir to
> the throne
> YOUNG PRINCE, 7, their youngest son
> CLARENCE, middle son of the Duchess of York
> RICHARD, Duke of Gloucester, youngest son of the
> Duchess of York

FUTURE ROYAL FAMILY
> HENRY RICHMOND, lieutenant-commander in the navy
> LORD STANLEY, air vice-marshal, Richmond's uncle
> GEORGE STANLEY, his son

CIVILIANS
> EARL RIVERS, Queen Elizabeth's brother
> DUKE OF BUCKINGHAM
> LORD HASTINGS, the Prime Minister
> LADY HASTINGS, his wife

SIR ROBERT BRACKENBURY, Governor of
The Tower
WILLIAM CATESBY, the monarch's permanent
private secretary
ARCHBISHOP
LORD MAYOR
CITY GENTLEMAN
JAILER AT THE TOWER

MILITARY

SERGEANT RATCLIFFE, Richard's batman
JAMES TYRELL, army corporal
NON-COMMISSIONED OFFICER, Tyrell's accomplice
NCO's WIFE
ADJUTANT, to Richmond
SUBALTERN, to Richard

CAPTION. This was only agreed once the film was complete. I should have preferred to do without it, as the long, wordless prologue (scenes 1–13) gradually introduces the faces of the principle players and hints at their relationships. Before Richard's first speech, it is important to understand that his story develops against the background of a civil war. The caption explains this rather less extensively than Shakespeare's *King Henry VI* trilogy about the Wars of the Roses! In the film, the less advance warning the better – enough for the audience to know that a rebel army is closing in on the reigning King.

scene 1 was devised by RL to establish the 1930s setting and to present the militaristic background to the civilian politics of the film. It has startling sound effects, no music and only a few scarcely distinguishable words.

The set of the country mansion was originally built and designed for a BBC TV production by our production designer Tony Burrough. Rather than throw them in the incinerator, Tony had rescued the walls of timber and canvas and, at his own cost, stored them for a rainy day in a warehouse in the north of England, whence they were brought south to Spitfire Studios in Middlesex and re-erected and furnished. This was a generous gift, as the set was to be destroyed on camera. Unless it's RL, I've never seen a harder worker than Tony.

He looked at various stately homes of England in which to film. He says: 'We decided they were too safe and we wanted to be brave. We were creating our own world, our own history of the 1930s and our invention of what might have happened if Britain had been involved in a civil war sixty years ago. We decided we wanted to find eccentric places and turn them into elements of the story.' (So the scenery was never to be just decoration and glamour for their own sakes.)

'We decided Victorian Gothic was a nice way of placing King Edward's court in a traditional context. When Richard takes over, he moves his headquarters away from the palace into accommodation derivative of Speer's Berlin or Mussolini's Rome.

'We drew on elements we liked about the look of the 1930s as they really were and used them as keys. The costumes, for example, were very specific to 1936. Shuna Harwood, the costume designer, scoured the vintage clothing stores of London and Paris for 30s originals. We're using 30s furniture and props and architecture that has survived from the 30s. The style of the picture, however, is heightened reality. We haven't been slavish to period detail. Some things which might not be accurate look perfect in context. That's the great thing about movies: you can cheat. We didn't compromise – Richard Loncraine is very uncompromising!'

CAPTION :

TWO POWERFUL FAMILIES ARE BATTLING
FOR CONTROL OF THE COUNTRY.

THE FIELD HEADQUARTERS OF THE KING'S ARMY

I   **INT. DRAWING-ROOM OF COUNTRY
MANSION – NIGHT**

In the countryside away from the capital, KING HENRY's
forces have requisitioned a small-scale stately home for their
temporary military headquarters.

The drawing-room is comfortable and traditionally decorated
– chintz combined with velvet and brocades. From the rose
of an ornately plastered ceiling hangs a discreet chandelier.
The mullioned windows are shuttered against spying eyes.
Coals burn red in the marbled fireplace.

Cables snake down the walls, bringing electricity for
telephones and lighting to the military occupants. Harsh, bare
lightbulbs. A large, operations map of England is pinned onto
a tapestry.

KING HENRY embraces his beloved son and heir,
PRINCE EDWARD, and retires for the night, through
double-doors to his makeshift, bedroom sanctuary. An armed
CORPORAL stands easy outside.

PRINCE EDWARD, with his long-haired RETRIEVER
for company, quietly settles down to a night of paperwork.
An ADJUTANT brings a tray with the Prince's supper.

PRINCE EDWARD sits at a large desk, illuminated by an
anglepoise lamp. As he eats, reads and makes notes, he adjusts
the position of the silver-framed photo of his beloved wife,
LADY ANNE.

As the tank's appearance could not be rehearsed nor repeated, four cameras filmed its one-and-only entrance. I suggested that the silence after its deafening arrival could be broken by footsteps of panic, preferably in time to the iambic pentameter thud of 'de-*dum*, de-*dum*, de-*dum*, de-*dum*, de-*dum*'. It was explained that panic is rarely regular. So, instead, I breathed rhythmically through the gas-mask. It is appropriate that Richard's face should at first sight be masked – as are his feelings from the world.

mumbling a prayer. 'holy king Henry' of the *Henry VI* trilogy.

There are soft sounds of normal, peaceful activity – scratch of PRINCE EDWARD's pen, scrape of fork on china, ticking of a grandfather clock. The only sense of war is the Morse code receiver clicking outside in the Hall.

The alert dog hears it first. An unidentifiable creaking rumble. Is it getting louder? PRINCE EDWARD looks up from his desk and rises to open a shutter and peer outside. The whimpering dog is more interested in the opposite outer wall. His sudden barking is drowned by an unholy roar.

PRINCE EDWARD turns – to see the entire wall cave in, as an army tank enters the drawing-room. Furniture is crushed and priceless plaster falls and chokes the air. Before he can react, a rifle shot splatters the back of his head across a painting of an idyllic rural scene. The GUARD and ADJUTANT are also shot.

Then the electricity fails and the lights go out. An explosion and a ball of fire backlight the tank lodged in the shattered wall.

Through the flames and the acrid smoke, RICHARD, DUKE OF GLOUCESTER, in full battle-gear and disguised by a gas mask, emerges from behind the tank, leading half a dozen COMMANDOS.

Two of PRINCE EDWARD's AIDES-DE-CAMP dash through from the Hall, to be promptly shot by the invaders. RICHARD checks that PRINCE EDWARD is safely dead, then moves over to the double-doors. He kicks them open. Kneeling, mumbling a prayer, is the old KING. He looks up, at the dark figure in the doorway. A burst from RICHARD's Sten gun and the old KING's frail body is thrown back across the bed by a hail of bullets.

The long civil war is over.

DOG. cf. 'dogs bark at me as I pass by them' (1.1).

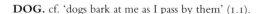

CREDITS. Music is heard for the first time as the credits are shown. In an earlier draft, the new royal family was seen on black-and-white newsreel, an idea we abandoned here but retained in scene 91.

scene 2. It was unnecessary to go to the expense of dressing-up London, when the more important point was to have a look at Richard. The simple shot of returning to civilian life took a couple of hours driving round the anonymous official buildings behind Whitehall, London. My car was loaded onto a larger vehicle which also pulled along the camera and crew.

scene 3 was filmed but RL judged it too confusing among all the other introductions to the principal characters. Lady Anne's first entrance is more effective where Shakespeare has it in the play, just before she meets Richard in scene 22.

scene 4. I had remembered from the theatre programmes of my youth 'Cigarettes by Abdulla' and made them Richard's preferred brand, not realising that they were no longer in production. Diligently, the property department located the six surviving packets of Abdulla in London and bought one of them intact. Even so, I smoked non-nicotine herbal cigarettes as, for this shot alone, I had to light about twenty one after the other. The 30s lighter showed its age and regularly refused to spark into life.

RICHARD turns into CAMERA. At his feet, the DOG
never stops howling.

CAPTION :

> 'RICHARD III'

CREDITS OVER the New Order as it prepares to celebrate
its victory.

2   **EXT. STREETS OF THE CAPITAL – DAY**

Led and followed by an escort of OUTRIDERS,
RICHARD's staff-car drives through some unidentifiable,
rubble-filled, war-torn streets of the capital, unnoticed by
CITIZENS dourly adjusting to normality.

SERGEANT RATCLIFFE, RICHARD's loyal batman, is at
the wheel. From the back seat, RICHARD looks straight
ahead, expressionless.

3   **INT. STAIRCASE – THE PALACE – DAY**

A young liveried FOOTMAN carries two of the heavier
bags; a middle-aged LADY-IN-WAITING grasps one
suitcase-handle in both her hands. LADY ANNE, in
mourning black, follows them down the long corridor,
banging her bags along the carpet and endangering the Ming
vases below the royal portraits, which dominate the walls.
This is no longer her home. A new dynasty is taking over.

4   **INT. RICHARD'S VEHICLE – DAY**

RICHARD's right hand selects an Abdulla from his
monogrammed, silver cigarette-case and lights up with the
ultimate in tasteful 30s lighters.

scene 5 was shot at Richmond Fellowship (built by Halsey Ricardo in 1906). The film shows little of the effect of politics on the general population (cf. the whole national view of *Henry IV parts 1 & 2*) – rather it is the backstage story of a powerful Establishment. Hence this domestic introduction of the new Queen and her son off-duty. Although he's not named in the dialogue, we had called him 'Prince James' on the cast-list, as confusingly his real name was 'Richard'.

scene 6. This reference to King Edward's lechery in preparation for Richard's accusations in scene 74 seemed unnecessarily confusing for the first time he is seen. It was more important to note his ailing health: cf. Richard's calumny of King Edward at the end of scene 48.

scene 7. This was my last piece of filming, on Sunday morning, 8 October 1995, five weeks after the principal photography was completed. We are on Lambeth Bridge across the Thames.

scene 8. The developing image is of three very different royal brothers – King Edward, Clarence and Richard.

5   INT. THE QUEEN'S BATHROOM – THE PALACE
     – DAY

Her Majesty, the American-born QUEEN ELIZABETH,
has only just moved into the Palace but already looks at
home. A LADY-IN-WAITING is trying to get her ready for
the evening but the new Queen, in her chic undies, is more
interested in her 7-year-old son PRINCE JAMES, who is
having his hair washed by his NANNY. The naughty Prince,
in nothing but his drawers, flicks water at his mother, who
shrieks with laughter.

6   INT. THE KING'S DRESSING-ROOM – THE
     PALACE – DAY

The new King, His Majesty KING EDWARD, half-dressed
for the Victory Ball, is in skittish mood but he has to take his
medicine. He is sitting at a dressing-table, with his VALET
standing behind and knotting the white bow-tie. KING
EDWARD offers his tongue, on which a nubile NURSE
tentatively places two blood-pressure pills. As KING
EDWARD swallows them down, with the aid of a tumbler
of Scotch-and-soda, the NURSE flinches. The royal hand is
working its way steadily up between her thighs beneath her
crisp starched frock.

7   EXT. RICHARD'S VEHICLE – DAY

RICHARD's car crosses a bridge on its way to the Palace, in
the distance, situated on the edge of the Thames.

8   INT. DARK ROOM – CLARENCE'S STUDIO –
     THE PALACE – DAY

CLARENCE, RICHARD's older brother, wearing an apron
over his dress-shirt, with bow-tie undone, removes a

scene 10. The Palace exterior is of St Pancras Chambers, designed by George Gilbert Scott (1868), which until 1935 was the Grand Midland Hotel at the rail terminus for trains going north. It has been removed by film-magic from Euston Road to the south bank of the Thames.

scene 11. The Queen's Quarters were found in the fantastically decorated Strawberry Hill House, which in 1748 Horace Walpole converted into a small Gothic castle on the Thames at Twickenham.

As Richard approaches the Duchess of York with a friendly greeting, she almost snubs him.

photograph from the developer and adds it to the row of family photographs pinned above him. He suddenly notices the time, takes off his steel-rimmed bifocals and hurries from the studio.

9   **INT. CLARENCE'S STUDIO – THE PALACE – DAY**

CLARENCE removes his apron, puts on a jacket, leaving his bow-tie undone, and walks across the room to get his Leica camera equipment and hurries out.

10   **EXT. COURTYARD – THE PALACE – EVENING**

Through the windows of the Palace façade, the chandeliers are being lit, as RICHARD's car and escort roar into view.

11   **INT. THE QUEEN'S QUARTERS – THE PALACE – EVENING**

KING EDWARD, QUEEN ELIZABETH and their son, the 7-year-old PRINCE JAMES, are now dressed to the nines. 15-year-old PRINCESS ELIZABETH, is a little nervous in her first ball-gown. KING EDWARD coughs asthmatically.

CLARENCE, now in evening dress, arrives, with his mother, the DUCHESS OF YORK, on his arm. She is, tiara-to-toe, an Edwardian matriarch and proudly curtsies to her eldest son, KING EDWARD.

PRINCESS ELIZABETH kisses her uncle and adjusts his ill-knotted white tie.

They are joined by RICHARD, magnificent in full dress uniform of the army's Commander-in-Chief. The Royal

scene 12 was filmed at Shoreham Aerodrome on the same day as scene 99. The airfield at Shoreham is the oldest public licensed airfield in the country still operating (1910). The terminal building was built in 1936.

In the play, Queen Elizabeth's Woodville Family are reviled by Richard as provincial outsiders to the metropolitan power-centre. A 30s equivalent was to make them American: witness the British Establishment's outcry in 1936, when King Edward VIII wanted Wallis Simpson to be his queen.

EARL RIVERS (whose title might be a credible first name) has to be established as an American visitor. An earlier draft had Rivers looking out of the window of his first-class cabin, as the aircraft was coming in to land. From his point of view, the city of the film was spread out below.

scene 13 shows a remnant of the interior grandeur of the old Hotel and a useful shot identifying the new royal family.

scene 14. We filmed on weekdays in a working church in West London, St Cuthbert's (designed by Hugh Romeo Gough in 1884) whose roof leaks. Some ecclesiastical statuary can be seen behind the royal dais.

Family is complete, as RICHARD bows to his brother, the King.

12 **EXT. PAN-AM TRANSATLANTIC PLANE –
EVENING**

EARL RIVERS, the new Queen's American brother, appears at the exit from the aeroplane, just landed from the USA. He grins at the PAN-AM AIR HOSTESS, who flashes her sexiest smile. In time to the jolly dance music on the soundtrack, the waggish playboy shakes off his jet-lag with a skip-and-a-dance down the stairs of the gangway.

He ends with a wave to the appreciative AIR HOSTESS, who waves back.

13 **INT. GRAND STAIRCASE – THE PALACE –
EVENING**

KING EDWARD, QUEEN ELIZABETH, PRINCE JAMES, PRINCESS ELIZABETH, the DUCHESS OF YORK and RICHARD are grouped on the landing of the grand staircase, overlooking the balustrade.

CLARENCE is on the landing below. He sets the self-timer, and runs up the stairs to join the family group photograph.

END OF CREDITS

14 **INT. BALLROOM – THE PALACE – NIGHT**

The Victory Ball is in full swing. 50 SERVANTS ply champagne to the 250 GUESTS.

scene 14. In my first draft, I had introduced the principal characters at a Guildhall Banquet given by the Lord Mayor of London in honour of King Edward and the victorious York family. RL was keen to avoid too many medieval settings and opted for a more private celebration onboard the royal yacht, as it steamed up the Thames. This would have involved the design and erection of a prohibitively expensive studio set.

PRINCESS ELIZABETH does not appear in the play and Richmond has to wait until act 5 scene 2 for his first entrance. Here the future king and queen clearly fancy each other – the sort of wholesomely sexy couple who make Richard feel inadequate. Richmond, born into the Establishment, moves confidently within the circles of power.

Duke of Buckingham and Richard Gloucester. We wanted these two allies to be associated with each other as early as possible. A previous idea was to introduce Buckingham in his workplace – an airline or newspaper-group headquarters, perhaps. Here he looks like an ornament at this important event.

How well can you ever know such a man? Maybe Buckingham retires each night to a lonely bed in Mayfair. Richard works out that Buckingham is greedy and greed is at the basis of their partnership. Not that Buckingham should need bribing to be involved as Richard's agent or kingmaker. He loves the sweet-talking and the civilised intrigue. Meanwhile they smile together.

The white-tuxedoed 20-PIECE BAND is at the climax of an Al Bowley set.

A foxtrot starts up and the smiling KING EDWARD leads his radiant QUEEN ELIZABETH onto the floor. KING EDWARD good-humouredly shows off a little fancy footwork.

LORD HASTINGS, the Prime Minister, is talking to the DUCHESS OF YORK, who sits upright on a gilt armchair. PRINCE JAMES is restless in his seat. PRINCESS ELIZABETH is entranced by the occasion, particularly when she is introduced to a dashing, young, naval officer, HENRY RICHMOND.

LORD STANLEY is present with his wife, LADY STANLEY, who is tending to their 6-year-old son, GEORGE.

Everyone is smiling and well-pleased. They'd never guess that the ever-observant RICHARD, Abdulla in hand, is less than happy. He has a smile and a handshake for all who pass by.

The imposing DUKE OF BUCKINGHAM, with cigar and brandy, greets RICHARD with a broad smile and immense self-confidence.

15   **EXT. COURTYARD – THE PALACE – NIGHT**

20 Rolls Royces are lined up. RATCLIFFE and the other liveried CHAUFFEURS are passing round the Craven As. Dance music continues from indoors.

EARL RIVERS steps out of his limousine, doffs his top-hat and looks up at the palatial façade. He whistles with admiration: Sis has done very well for herself. He is fulsomely greeted by the MAJOR DOMO, who has been waiting for him at the front door.

scene 16. Shakespeare included nearly a hundred songs in his plays, although there are none in *Richard III*. I scoured these and his 154 love sonnets to find a lyric that might be appropriate for a 30s pastiche. The lyrics which were chosen are by Christopher Marlowe but have been attributed to Shakespeare.

> Come live with me and be my love
> And we will all the pleasures prove . . .

The Victory Ball was shot in only two days, after which I couldn't get Trevor Jones' catchy 30s tune out of my head. It had been pre-recorded and relayed over and over, as Stacey Kent mimed to her own voice.

I asked for Shakespeare's initials to be on the dance-band's music stands. I liked Colin Good's resemblance to a young Jack Payne or Glen Miller.

'sun of York' is an ironic triple pun, referring to two sons of the victorious York Family – the new King Edward and his commander-in-chief, Richard himself.

58

16 INT. BALLROOM – THE PALACE – NIGHT

RICHARD moves slowly through the throng.

Everyone watches delightedly as the little PRINCE JAMES dances on his mother's toes.

CLARENCE is taking snaps.

The QUEEN suddenly spots her brother EARL RIVERS and sweeping the young prince up in her arms, she rushes to greet him.

SIR WILLIAM CATESBY, the monarch's permanent private secretary, leans over KING EDWARD's chair and they look toward CLARENCE, whose photography is interrupted by an urgent, private request from LIEUTENANT SIR ROBERT BRACKENBURY, in Chief Constable's uniform. TWO MILITARY STRONGMEN, looking uncomfortable in civilian evening dress, are in attendance.

As CLARENCE is politely led away, he looks toward his brother KING EDWARD, who asthmatically coughs and turns his attention back to the jovial RIVERS, who is now seated with the royal party. Apart from CATESBY and the royal brothers, KING EDWARD and RICHARD, everyone seems to have missed the whole episode.

RICHARD watches his brother CLARENCE being led out. Then he skirts round the dancers, to have a word with the BAND LEADER. The music ends with a flourish and the Royals settle in their seats. The whole company turns toward RICHARD, as he clears his throat and scratches the mesh of the singer's microphone.

> RICHARD
> **Now is the winter of our discontent**
> **Made glorious summer by this sun of York!**

RICHARD's first speech begins as a public announcement. By using a measured and slightly declamatory tone, I wanted to draw attention to the formality of language appropriate to public address, even in a modern setting, in the hope that the ear might quickly be attuned to Shakespeare's verse. *Richard III* is certainly a talkie, in which the words are paramount.

'And all the clouds that loured upon our house . . .' With the repeated 'ow's and 'm's, Richard draws attention to his oratorical skills.

'Delightful measures' was the clue that we should see a dance, in which Richard does not participate.

'and now . . .' The camera moves in for a big close-up revealing Richard's rotten lower-teeth and his discoloured left eye as the mood of the speech changes.

'barbed steeds' are the cavalry's armoured horses, suggesting Richard's romantic view of war. Horses later appear throughout the battle scenes.

RICHARD toasts the smiling, new King. KING EDWARD regally acknowledges the laughter and applause of his family, friends and national leaders from politics and commerce.

>   RICHARD
>   (continuing)
> **And all the clouds that loured upon our house**
> **In the deep bosom of the ocean buried.**
> **Now are our brows bound with victorious**
>   **wreaths;**
> **Our bruised arms hung up for monuments;**
> **Our stern alarums changed to merry meetings,**
> **Our dreadful marches to delightful measures.**

APPLAUSE as RICHARD smiles. The popular war-leader is working well in these civilian surroundings.

HASTINGS smiles, satisfied; the ARCHBISHOP looks benignly content.

The appreciative audience misses RICHARD's irony, with the exception of BUCKINGHAM, who listens intently and quizzically, puffing on his Havana and sipping his Napoleon 5-star.

>   RICHARD
>   (continuing)
> **Grim-visaged war has smoothed his wrinkled**
>   **front:**
> **And now, instead of mounting barbed steeds,**
> **To fight the souls of fearful adversaries**
> **He . . .**

scene 17 is set in an ante-room at Strawberry Hill House, refurnished with plastic urinals and washbasin – a private place where Richard could look at himself in a mirror. My first idea had been to see Richard alone, talking in front of a three-sided mirror in his bedroom. My second had him leaving the Ball via the Palace Mews, where Ratcliffe was waiting to drive him to The Tower and where he first spies Tyrell, the stable-lad, grooming Richard's beloved horses. My third, if the Ball were onboard the royal yacht, put Richard in the most private of places, the loo of the royal retiring accommodation.

'To the lascivious pleasing of a lute.' The repeated 'l's trip off the tongue, as the speech turns from rhetoric to a confessional tone. We have just seen King Edward capering nimbly on the dance-floor.

At the RNT, this opening speech was spoken directly to the audience to intensify their identification with the speaker; a powerful asset which Shakespeare generally reserves for his leading characters. In the play, there is an effective group of adjacent monologues from Buckingham (4.2), Tyrell (4.3) and Queen Margaret (4.4). In the film the device is reserved for Richard. Without it, the audience might find it hard to engage sympathetically with a man so bent on ill-doings. Similarly the troubled and troublesome inner natures of Iago, Leontes and Macbeth are revealed in their soliloquies.

In the theatre, audiences welcome a character who steps out of the action of the drama to address them, whether in Shakespeare, a pantomime or a musical. On the television screen, talking heads are so familiar that a Shakespeare soliloquy works well. The rule of traditional film-making is that actors should never look at the camera – a convention which is riskier to break through than the fourth wall of a proscenium stage.

I never doubted that I should challenge the naturalism of cinema by talking to the camera.

17 INT. WASHROOM – THE PALACE – NIGHT

RICHARD flings open the door of the stately lavatory and makes for the WC cubicle, past the ornate, carved mirrors above the deep washstands, with their gold taps and luxurious selection of towels, brushes, soaps and lotions. In the distance, the DANCE BAND plays 'A Delightful Measure'.

>   RICHARD
>   (continuing)
> . . . capers nimbly in a lady's chamber,
> To the lascivious pleasing of a lute.
> But I, that am not shaped for sportive tricks,
> Nor made to court an amorous looking-glass,
> I, that am rudely stamped –
> Deformed, unfinished, sent before my time
> Into this breathing world, scarce half made up,
> And that so lamely and unfashionable
> That dogs bark at me, as I halt by them:

RICHARD pulls the chain and emerges to wash his hand.

>   RICHARD
>   (continuing)
> Why, I, in this weak piping time of peace,
> Have no delight to pass away the time,
> Unless to spy my shadow in the sun,
> And descant on my own deformity.

RICHARD looks in the mirror at his blasted, sagging, left profile, the Brylcreemed hair smooth over his alopeciaed dome. He dries his right hand . . .

'Why, I can smile; and murder while I smile;
And wet my cheeks with artificial tears
And frame my face to all occasions!'
I included these lines from Richard of Gloucester's speech in *Henry VI part 3* (3.2).
Olivier's screenplay plundered more. Richard is not a cry-baby but he will weep
twice in the film – by design with Lady Anne and for real after his nightmare on
the eve of battle.

'I cannot prove a lover . . .' Richard's wooing of Lady Anne in scene 23 may
seem to contradict this confession. I preferred to take it literally – that Richard has
had little success with sex, because he doubts anyone could find him physically
attractive and has devoted himself exclusively to his career as a full-time soldier.

'hate the idle pleasures of these days.' Richard allies himself with other
military malcontents, like Don John in *Much Ado About Nothing* who takes revenge
on society for his bastardy just as Richard does for his deformity.

scene 19. This pier-head is just across the road from the palace of the Archbishop
of Canterbury in Lambeth, south London. In the distance are the Houses of
Parliament, one of the few London landmarks glimpsed in the film. The structure
of the pier was a little decorated with Gothic shapes.

Although the River Police had given their permission, one of their boats sped
across as we filmed, to complain that our arc-lights might dazzle the navigators of
the tourist boats and the occasional barge collecting waste upstream. Fortunately
there was little river traffic that night and we didn't have to wait long for it to pass.

                    RICHARD
                    (continuing; his lips scarcely move as he
                    addresses both himself and the CAMERA
                    through the mirror)
          Why, I can smile; and murder while I smile;
          And wet my cheeks with artificial tears
          And frame my face to all occasions!
          And, therefore, since I cannot prove a lover,
          I am determined to prove a villain
          And hate the idle pleasures of these days.
          Plots have I laid . . .

18   **INT. WALKWAY – THE PALACE – NIGHT**

As RICHARD returns to the celebrations he looks down
from the cast-iron walkway that leads back to the ballroom.

                    RICHARD
                    (continuing to CAMERA)
          To set my brothers, Clarence and the King,
          In deadly hate, the one against the other.

19   **EXT. LANDING STAGE/MILITARY LAUNCH –**
      THE PALACE – NIGHT

Far below on the stone steps of the Thames Embankment
RICHARD spies his brother CLARENCE, with
BRACKENBURY and ESCORT, as he is led down to a
waiting launch.

20   **INT. WALKWAY – THE PALACE – NIGHT**

RICHARD watches, turns and walks away.

scene 21. The standard practice is to shoot a scene from a number of angles. A 'master-shot' showing all the action can then be inter-cut with closer shots of the speakers. This scene, however, was filmed from just one angle.

RL often opted for a single set-up which continues throughout a scene, because it gives the actors a chance to control the pace and the changing moods. Anyway, he wasn't given enough time in the ten-week shooting schedule for the luxury of a number of set-ups. He kept in his head the way the film would eventually be cut together and only shot what was necessary; a discipline he has perfected in his filming of commercials. Of the 500 set-ups in *Richard III*, the editor, Paul Green, had to discard only eight.

Each new set-up involves re-lighting. I'm often resentful of the time permitted for the essential preparation of camera positioning and lighting the set and faces. That done, the actors seem to be expected to get it right without delay whilst producers look at their watches and frown. But I could never have resented the wait while Peter Biziou dextrously painted the air with light. By walkie-talkie or whispers or sign language, he communicated with his chief gaffer, Peter Bloor, and the assistant electricians who lugged, stabilised and plugged-in for action the lamps behind the camera. From the day we met at my make-up test, Peter was encouraging: initially because he agreed to take the job – he is in great demand – and to the end, because he enthused about performances and direction and about his own satisfaction in being involved.

21 **EXT. PALACE – LANDING STAGE/MILITARY LAUNCH – NIGHT**

RICHARD emerges from the dark tunnel that leads to the Palace landing stage.

> RICHARD
> (continuing; calling over to CLARENCE)
> **Brother! What means this armed guard?**

RICHARD hurries to CLARENCE down the slippery stone steps.

> CLARENCE
> **His Majesty,**
> **Tendering my person's safety, has appointed**
> **This conduct, to convey me to the Tower.**

> RICHARD
> **But what is the matter, Clarence, may I know?**

> CLARENCE
> **Yes, Richard, when I know; but I protest**
> **As yet, I do not.**

> RICHARD
> **Why this it is, when men are ruled by women!**
> **It's not the King that sends you to the Tower.**
> **Elizabeth the Queen, Clarence, it's she.**
> **We are not safe, brother. We are not safe.**

> BRACKENBURY
> **I beseech your Lordships both to pardon me.**
> **His Majesty has strictly given me charge**
> **That no man shall have private conference –**
> **Of what degree so-ever – with your brother.**

'Brother, farewell.'

In the play, Clarence has a young son and daughter. In the film, he is a childless bachelor, as simple and plain as his brother Richard is devious. He has withdrawn from the political life of his two brothers and has a job elsewhere, in some world of academics or artists. RL, who collects cameras, decided Clarence should be an amateur photographer, recording his surroundings without noticing what's going on until it is too late. Right up to his death, Clarence is fooled by Richard's bonhomie.

Nigel Hawthorne is a master of irony and British sang-froid, witness the *Yes Minister* television series (1980–7). As Clarence, he played on the other side of his own personality, warmly and wistfully.

BRACKENBURY invites CLARENCE on board the
military police launch moored in the river.

>#### RICHARD
>**We speak no treason, Brackenbury. We say**
> **the King**
>**Is wise and virtuous and his Queen –**
>**Well-struck in years.**

>#### BRACKENBURY
>(refusing to be amused)
>**I do beseech you both to pardon me.**

>#### CLARENCE
>**We know your charge, Brackenbury, and**
> **will obey.**

>#### RICHARD
>(hugging CLARENCE)
>**We are the Queen's subjects, and must obey.**
>**Brother, farewell. I will unto the King.**
>**Meanwhile, this deep disgrace in brotherhood**
>**Touches me deeper than you can imagine.**

>#### CLARENCE
>**I know it pleases neither of us well.**

>#### RICHARD
>**Well, your imprisonment shall not be long.**
>**I will deliver you, or else lie for you.**
>**Meantime have patience.**

CLARENCE ironically holds up his handcuffs.

>#### CLARENCE
>**I must perforce. Farewell.**

'Simple, plain Clarence.' This scene is full of ironies, as Richard lies his way through. His adrenalin gleefully pumping, he can hardly wait to share his deviousness with the audience. Then off he springs to give the performance of his life, as he woos Lady Anne: from a parody of brotherly love to a parody of courtship.

scene 22. At the RNT, Bob Crowley's hanging line of overhead lamp-shades indicated a mortuary corridor, with three orderlies in charge of the corpse on its hospital trolley. We filmed in the abandoned Pearl Assurance Building (designed by Mokton, 1912) on the edge of the City of London in Holborn. On either side of the corridor in this scene, there are heavy steel doors which can still be opened on to the cell-like safes where securities and valuables were once locked up and guarded.

scene 23. A defunct lower-floor storage-room was turned into a basement mortuary by foreshortening the windows with plasterboard and paint. I love the details of film-sets, all ready, if necessary, for a camera close-up. One joke was not filmed. On the long mortuary wall at the back, there were dummy refrigerator doors, labelled with the surnames of Shakespeare's contemporary rivals – Dekker, Greene, Jonson, Kyd, Marlowe, Marston and Massinger.

RICHARD looks down from the quay and takes out a large, white handkerchief, to dry his sniffles. He waves to CLARENCE, as the launch speeds cross-stream, out toward the sinister silhouette of the menacing Tower on the opposite embankment. The moonlight glitters on the grey water.

> RICHARD
> **Simple, plain Clarence! I do love you so,**
> **That I shall shortly send your soul to Heaven –**
> **If Heaven will take the present from my hands!**
> (blowing his nose)
> **And then, I'll marry . . .**
> **What though I killed her husband? And his**
> **father?**

22 INT. CORRIDOR – PUBLIC HOSPITAL – DAY

The messy aftermath of civil conflict. The corridor is crammed with the sick and dying. LADY ANNE is elegant in her mourning black but distraught and scarcely recognised in headscarf and dark glasses, as she glides through the crush.

WIDOWS and fatherless FAMILIES wait for confirmation of their menfolk's deaths. The SICK AND WOUNDED overflow from the adjacent wards. LADY ANNE pushes open the double swing-doors to the mortuary.

23 INT. MORTUARY – PUBLIC HOSPITAL – DAY

Through the opaque glass tiles of the ceiling, cathedral-like sunbeams fall onto the tiled walls and marble floor of the underground chamber. Cold and quiet after the confusion outside.

Three white-coated HOSPITAL ORDERLIES are

PRINCE EDWARD. In the play, Lady Anne accompanies her father-in-law's corpse to its burial. In the film, his son is recognisable on the morgue's marble slab. Olivier's film made the same substitution. The war in which the Prince was killed has been over long enough for the new regime to celebrate its victory but his corpse is not yet buried and Lady Anne's grief is still at its height. Shakespeare's time-scale is only confusing when you analyse its inconsistencies.

'If ever he have wife . . .' In the background, Richard silently emerges from behind Lady Anne, his future wife, at the moment when she curses herself-to-be.

'black magician . . .' In the play, there are other references to necromancy. Richard bases his slanderous charge against Clarence on the witness of a wizard; he calls Queen Margaret a 'foul wrinkled witch'; he blames his deformity on 'damned witchcraft'. If this is thought to be outlandishly medieval for the 1930s, there have been many modern world leaders in thrall to astrology, from Hitler to Reagan.

'happy earth . . .' Richard notes to himself that Lady Anne's particular happiness lies not just in love but in being married to the late heir-to-the-throne, with the promise of influence and riches as his consort. She does not need to have it explained in words, that a liaison with Richard would lead her back to those privileges: cf. the youthful widow Jackie Kennedy's marriage to Aristotle Onassis.

attending to the corpse of PRINCE EDWARD on its
marble plinth. His wounds have been sewn up and tidied.
Scalpels and other surgical implements are at hand.
Prominent is an empty coffin on a gurney.

The shock of her husband's death has now released LADY
ANNE's grief and anger. Her mascara has run down her pale
make-up. She gestures to the ORDERLIES to leave
her alone.

> LADY ANNE
> **O, cursed be the hand that made these holes;**
> **Cursed the heart that had the heart to do it;**
> **Cursed the blood that let this blood from hence!**
> **If ever he have child, abortive be it.**
> **If ever he have wife, let her be made**
> **More miserable by the life of him,**
> **Than I am made by my young husband's death.**

RICHARD has been watching through the glass panels of
the doors. LADY ANNE hears the door open and turns to
see RICHARD.

> LADY ANNE
> **What black magician conjures up this fiend,**
> **To stop devoted charitable deeds?**

> RICHARD
> **Sweet saint, for charity be not so cursed.**

> LADY ANNE
> **Foul devil, for God's sake hence and trouble**
> **   me not;**
> **For you have made the happy earth my hell.**

RICHARD does not move. LADY ANNE, unnerved by his
gaze, tries to shame him into a response.

In the foreground of this establishing shot of the mortuary as Lady Anne walks in, there are two battle-torn extras, genuine amputees. In an early draft, the wooing was set over the King's corpse as it lay in state, next to the new mausoleum to his son, Lady Anne's husband.

On the page, it seems incredible that Lady Anne would ever succumb to her husband's killer. In performance, the scene (1.2) is invariably convincing. Lady Anne's emotional juices are in full flood, as her grief and anger turn to curiosity and the need to be involved with the world once more. She is not out of control and Richard has to work hard to melt away her scathing wit with his sincerity. He plays too on her vanity and declares that his love for her led him to murder the men he should have taken prisoner. He even offers to kill himself, with conviction.

LADY ANNE
(continuing)
If you delight to *see* your heinous deed.
Behold this pattern of your butchery.

RICHARD acknowledges the man he has killed.

RICHARD
(soothingly)
Lady, you know no rules of charity.

LADY ANNE
Villain, *you* know no law of God nor man.

RICHARD
Vouchsafe, divine perfection of a woman,
Of this supposed crime to give me leave,
By circumstance, but to acquit myself.

LADY ANNE
Did you not kill my husband?

RICHARD
I grant you, yes.

LADY ANNE
D'you grant me, hedgehog? Then God grant
  me, too,
You may be damned for that wicked deed!

RICHARD
Gentle Lady Anne –

LADY ANNE
O, *he* was gentle, mild and virtuous.

'Your bedchamber.' Kristin Scott Thomas did not want to hear this as it would lessen the later shock of Richard's approach which makes her spit. It does not disrupt the flow nor make Richard's sincerity any less convincing, when whispered in confidence to the camera – one of the very few brief 'asides' other than the full-length monologues. Richard likes an audience to appreciate his ingenuity. In the play, the wooing is silently witnessed by Tressel and Berkeley and by the undertakers who attend to the corpse.

'These nails should rend that beauty from my cheeks!' Lady Anne accepts that she is beautiful – at least, she does not deny it. Even as she lambasts him, she is susceptible to Richard's flattery.

'He who bereft you, Lady, of your husband . . .' The audacity of the soothing euphemism and the mocking repetition of 'husband' always made theatre audiences laugh.

RICHARD

The fitter for the King of Heaven who has him.

LADY ANNE

And you unfit for any place but Hell!

RICHARD

Yes, one place else, if you will hear me name it.

LADY ANNE

Some dungeon.

RICHARD

(to himself)

Your bedchamber.

(out loud)

Let's leave this keen encounter of our wits.

Your beauty, that did haunt me in my sleep,

Could make me undertake the death of all

   the world,

So I might live one hour in your sweet bosom.

LADY ANNE

If I thought that, I tell you, homicide,

These nails should rend that beauty from

   my cheeks!

RICHARD

My eyes could not endure that beauty's wreck.

As all the world is cheered by the sun,

So I by that – it is my day, my life!

He who bereft you, Lady, of your husband,

Did it to help you to a better husband.

LADY ANNE spits. This is a point of no return.

However satisfying it may be to spit contempt at her enemy, she is shocked by her own vulgarity and is silent while Richard weeps and tells his tale. He makes no complaint. The thrill of this slow-motion chase is that the stoat never underestimates the rabbit and takes no chances. Richard's energy, as befits an active soldier, flows through each moment as if it were a matter of his life and death.

As they stare each other out. In the screenplay, particularly in this final version, I was encouraged to fill out the moments between the dialogue with some indication as to the passionate inner lives of the characters, so that their stories would be clear to those readers who were more used to scripts which are not by Shakespeare and in which action and explosions sound louder than words. I do not like inhibiting and restricting notes on acting from playwrights when they are written into their scripts as stage directions: but this screenplay is not intended to be an acting script.

LADY ANNE

His better does not breathe upon the earth.

RICHARD

He lives who loves you better than he could.

LADY ANNE

Where is he?

RICHARD

Here.

LADY ANNE spits full in RICHARD's face. He glares
murderously back at her. She recoils from his anger. But this
is not the first time that the deformed RICHARD has been
openly despised. She cannot bring herself to apologise or,
quite, to feel sorry for his half-pathetic expression.

As they stare each other out, a young, helpless widow and
the man old enough to be her protective father, there is a
sexual alarm in the space between them.

At last, RICHARD wipes his face dry, with his white
handkerchief.

RICHARD
(continuing; softly, almost forgiving)
Why do you spit at me?

LADY ANNE
(recovering her self-control)
Would it were mortal poison, for your sake.

RICHARD
Never came poison from so sweet a place.

'blind with weeping.' cf. 'I can . . . wet my cheeks with artificial tears' (scene 16). Richard is able to cry convincingly by recalling previous occasions when he has been hurt by revulsion from his appearance.

To dry my eyes, I used the same white handkerchief which waved-off Clarence to The Tower (scene 21).

'I humbly beg for death, upon my knee.' Richard inspires himself by playing the fantasy role of romantic lover. In the mirror he has razored a moustache of screen heroes like Clark Gable, Clifton Webb, David Niven, Douglas Fairbanks. When his declaration of love is rejected, Don Juan kneels to be punished, kneels to commit hari-kari at the executioner's block and simultaneously kneels to ask for her hand in marriage. Not all women would fall for it and, watching the film, I can never quite catch the moment when Lady Anne is won over. She never quite remembers herself (scene 73).

'No, do not pause –' 'Nay' Shakespeare wrote and as in the north of England we still use the word, I had to be convinced, mainly by myself, that there should be no irksome hooks on which audiences could hang their impatience with a text they found initially difficult to understand. All the 'thou's and 'thee's of my childhood have gone too. Shakespeare makes no distinction between 'thou' and 'you' that I can tell.

LADY ANNE

Never hung poison on a fouler toad.
Out of my sight! You do infect my eyes.

RICHARD
(he is crying now)
Those eyes of yours from mine have drawn
  salt tears.
But when I heard the story of my father's death
And all the standers-by had wet their cheeks,
Like trees bedashed with rain, in that sad time,
My manly eyes did scorn a humble tear:
And what that sorrow could not thence exhale,
Your beauty has and made them blind with
  weeping.
Teach not your lip such scorn, for it was made
For kissing, Lady, not for such contempt.

LADY ANNE is moved by this confession and RICHARD
risks offering to kiss her. But no: LADY ANNE turns away.

RICHARD
(continuing)
If your revengeful heart cannot forgive,
I humbly beg for death, upon my knee.

RICHARD takes the nearest, sharpest scalpel and hands it to
LADY ANNE.

RICHARD
(continuing)
No, do not pause – it was I who killed your
  husband;
But it was your heavenly face that set me on.

LADY ANNE almost dares to stab him but she is too

Kristin Scott Thomas as Lady Anne was much more than another name to boast of on the marquee. Acting with her was always instructive. Our analysis of this scene in rehearsal was inconclusive – RL uncertain whether Lady Anne's submission could be believable; I convinced that it could; and Kristin listening, head on one side, and grimacing wryly that perhaps a woman knew best. In front of the camera she embodied the character's emotions with an intensity that reminded me of Meryl Streep's enviable ability to forget herself as soon as the camera turns. Kristin's special quality onscreen is to encapsulate and minimise her naturally volatile expression of personality, without losing any of its variety. Subtle as she is in close-up, she is equally aware of the effect of her body's silhouette in long-shot as in scene 44.

RICHARD places the blade to his throat. Richard uses a handy scalpel. In the play (1.2) he lays his 'true breast naked to the deadly stroke' of his sword. This would indicate that Shakespeare was presenting the one and only time when undressing is in order. Onstage, I removed hat, gloves, greatcoat, Sam Browne's trappings, jacket and undid the collarless shirt to give Lady Anne a glimpse of the naked flesh that was so close to the spine's deformity and was hers to explore. As I was nightly aware that this was an actor's trick, mine as much as Richard's, I was almost relieved when RL didn't want me to repeat it in the film.

confused. Why is her enemy so attractive? She drops the scalpel and it clatters onto the floor.

> RICHARD
> (continuing)
> **Take up the blade again – or take up *me*.**

RICHARD offers the blade to LADY ANNE but she will not take it from him.

> LADY ANNE
> **I will not be your executioner.**

> RICHARD
> **Then, bid me kill myself and I will do it.**

> LADY ANNE
> **I have already.**

> RICHARD
> **That was in your rage. Speak it again.**

> LADY ANNE
> **I would I knew your heart.**

RICHARD places the blade to his throat. A drop of blood trickles from the glistening blade.

> LADY ANNE
> **I fear that it is false.**

> RICHARD
> **Then never was man true.**

> LADY ANNE
> **Well, well, put down the blade.**

'Vouchsafe to wear this ring.' Richard performs a crude marriage ceremony between beauty and the beast. Lady Anne can have few illusions that he will turn into a prince to rival her first husband. In the play, there is no direct reference to the marriage until Richard and Anne become King and Queen. She only re-appears to meet the other royal women immediately before the Coronation (4.1). She is overwhelmed by sadness and is impervious to other feelings by then. She has even smaller joy than her predecessor in 'being this country's queen'. She is childless although the historical Anne had a son who died aged ten.

Despite considerable cutting of lines throughout this scene, each step in Richard's seduction remains. In the film, Lady Anne appears in nine more scenes than in the play – most of them silently. This prepares for her heart-breaking confession, which is divided between scenes 73 and 93. It also steadily charts Richard's inadequacy as a husband. In marriage, he behaves as callously as he does elsewhere.

RICHARD
But shall I live in hope?

LADY ANNE
All men I hope live so . . .

At that ambiguous half-promise, RICHARD lets drop the
scalpel. He slowly lifts his right hand to his mouth and, with
his teeth, pulls off his family signet-ring.

RICHARD
Vouchsafe to wear this ring.

RICHARD slides the ring, wet with saliva, onto her
engagement finger.

LADY ANNE
To take is not to give.

RICHARD
(whispers)
May I, with all expedient duty, see you?

LADY ANNE looks at the contrite RICHARD. Her grief
has turned to open fascination.

LADY ANNE
And much it joys me too,
To see you are become so penitent.

RICHARD
(as he leaves)
Bid me farewell.

scene 24. Onstage, having undressed enough to show Lady Anne my chest, I put everything back on as quickly as I could, single-handed, meanwhile talking to the audience. Then I marched off to a score or two of tailors. All that survives of this cheeky theatricality is the final wriggling-on of his leather glove, as Richard solemnly climbs the stairs from the mortuary.

scene 25. This celebratory soliloquy of triumph is properly outrageous and breaks through the convention of naturalism as effortlessly as a song in a musical. Richard, who will never be so carefree again, dares to speak his mind and boast even within hearing of hospital patients, staff and visitors, all of whom are too preoccupied to notice him dancing through.

LADY ANNE
'Tis no more than you deserve;
But since you teach me how to flatter you,
Imagine I have said farewell already.

RICHARD turns and walks out into the corridor.

24   **INT. CORRIDOR – PUBLIC HOSPITAL – DAY**

RICHARD pauses outside the double-doors to
the mortuary.

RICHARD
(to himself)
Was ever woman in this humour wooed?
(to CAMERA)
Was ever woman in this humour won?

25   **INT. STAIRS – PUBLIC HOSPITAL – DAY**

RICHARD starts up the stairs.

RICHARD
(continuing, to CAMERA)
I'll have her. But I will not keep her long.
What? I, who killed her husband and his father,
To take her in her heart's extremest hate,
With curses in her mouth, tears in her eyes,
And yet to win her – all the world to nothing.
Ha!

RICHARD pauses, then strides down the corridor.

'I'll entertain some score or two of tailors . . .' Forty tailors indeed! In an interim screenplay, I unnecessarily illustrated these words with a visit to a tailor's shop, where Richard was measured and fitted for his new civilian wardrobe. On his way out, he tipped a war veteran begging in Savile Row.

'Shine out, fair sun . . .' The end of the scene is marked with the flourish of a rhyming couplet. It sent me prancing up the curving stairs. On the take used in the film, I spontaneously paused at the top, for another full-stop to the scene, a clenched fist flung in the air before leaving round the corner.

scene 27. In the dubbing studio was added 'Catesby!' from Queen Elizabeth, her first word in the film. It introduces the King's permanent private secretary, which was how he was played at the RNT. Tim McInnerny gives a convincing inner life to the sour looks and gliding gait of a senior representative of the Civil Service.

KING EDWARD. John Wood's career began supporting the young Richard Burton in three Shakespeare seasons at the Old Vic. He has played Richard III twice, first as an undergraduate at Oxford (1953) and then for the RNT (1979). For a time, he was indispensible to any new Tom Stoppard play. We played together in *Every Good Boy Deserves Favour*, Stoppard's collaboration with André Previn. On Broadway, John had already triumphed as Guildenstern and in *Travesties*. After *Richard III*, his next film (and mine) was *Rasputin* (HBO).

CLARENCE's Royal Pardon. Later, King Edward will refer to this order in scene 47. Under Richard's influence, he had issued an earlier order that Clarence should be executed. In this scene he issues a pardon. Scene 29 follows silently on, as Richard reads and destroys the countermand.

26   INT. UPPER CORRIDOR – PUBLIC HOSPITAL –
      DAY

                    RICHARD
                    (continuing)
          Upon my life she finds, although I cannot,
          Myself to be a marvellous proper man.
          I'll entertain some score or two of tailors
          To study fashions to adorn my body.
                    (half-singing)
          Shine out, fair sun, till I have bought a glass,
          That I may see my shadow as I pass.

Immaculate once more, RICHARD strides out. The sun
throws his shadow back onto the marble floor.

27   INT. THE KING'S LIBRARY – THE PALACE –
      DAY

Heavy early Victorian décor.

KING EDWARD is at his desk, his well-worn face the
victim of asthma, blood-pressure and general over-
indulgence.

QUEEN ELIZABETH is leaning over his shoulder
approvingly as he signs an official paper. CATESBY has
prepared the sealing wax for the Royal Seal.

KING EDWARD hands CATESBY the completed missive.
QUEEN ELIZABETH smiles with relief that
CLARENCE's Royal Pardon is on its way.

As CATESBY leaves with a bow, KING EDWARD starts a
serious cough. CATESBY turns, very worried, and QUEEN
ELIZABETH tries to help her husband. CATESBY rings the

scene 28. The undercroft of the chapel in Lincoln's Inn Fields, where lawyers train and work, has vaulted arches that are open to the air. These were glazed, creating a unique royal breakfast-room, furnished by the new Queen Elizabeth with gold-fish tank, chintz and a family atmosphere.

All Annette Bening's scenes were shot together within three weeks at the beginning of the schedule. Warren Beatty boosted all our spirits when he came to visit her on the set for this scene. Ten years before, he had troubled to call RL, whom he had never met, to congratulate him on his direction of *The Missionary*. When we needed to break all the Hollywood etiquette rules of agents, managements and personal representatives by contacting Annette quickly and directly, RL called the old Beatty number and Warren answered. Mrs Beatty read the script the minute it reached her (another broken rule of some stars – 'keep 'em sweating'). She at once agreed to play Queen Elizabeth and I've been grateful and delighted ever since. I know she was glad to return to Shakespeare which she had played during her time at the American Conservatory Theater in San Francisco.

bell for further assistance. The NURSE rushes in to attend her patient.

28   **INT. THE QUEEN'S QUARTERS – THE PALACE – DAY**

QUEEN ELIZABETH's taste is reflected in every knick-knack and pattern of the newly furnished apartments. A clock strikes 10 and then tick-tocks. Breakfast is served in the conservatory leading onto the Palace gardens. The summer morning sunlight filters through the trees outside.

QUEEN ELIZABETH is *déshabillé*, a champagne-glass in her manicured, be-ringed hand.

RIVERS is brunching on orange juice, black coffee and Danish.

At his own small table, the well-behaved PRINCE JAMES is absorbed with a boiled egg and toast-soldiers. The adults speak low, so as not to distract him.

> QUEEN ELIZABETH
> **The King is sickly, weak and melancholy.**

> RIVERS
> (joining her at the window)
> **Have patience, Sister.**
> **There's no doubt His Majesty**
> **Will soon recover his accustomed health.**

> QUEEN ELIZABETH
> **But his physicians fear him mightily.**
> **If he were dead, what would become of me?**

'O they are young . . .' reveals the worried, doting mother in juxtaposition to the carefree hostess who has been seen dancing with her little son on her toes. It is always revealing to spy public figures off-duty.

RIVERS. Before he speaks, spot the clues that Rivers is American. Off the Pan American flight he, in a republican sort of way, drops his gift-wrapped bundles into His Majesty's lap. Here he reads the *Wall Street Journal* and is dressed up in the cowboys-and-Indians kit he brought for his little nephew. Robert Downey Jr effortlessly conjured up a loose-limbed 30s playboy destined to be an early, rather pathetic victim of Richard's ambition.

I originally thought that an alternative would have been a more worldly wise, over-confident heavyweight like Robert Duvall or Gene Hackman, ready to take on the world by controlling his sister's newly royal destiny. Rivers does not have enough lines for that interpretation to be convincingly developed.

'My love, what danger can befall to you . . . ?'

RIVERS

**The heavens have blessed you with two
    goodly sons,
To be your comforters when he is gone.**

QUEEN ELIZABETH
(dropping the bombshell)

**O they are young and their minority
Is put into the trust of Richard Gloucester –
A man who loves not me, nor you,
    dear brother.**

RIVERS

Is it confirmed he will be Lord Protector?

QUEEN ELIZABETH

If the King miscarry . . .

KING EDWARD is at the doorway, helped by PRINCESS
ELIZABETH. He belies his illness by his confident manner.

KING EDWARD

**My love, what danger can befall to you
So long as Edward is your constant friend?
And a sovereign, whom Richard must obey?
Yes, whom he *shall* obey – and love you too.**

KING EDWARD and QUEEN ELIZABETH embrace
each other.

RIVERS thoughtfully sips his coffee.

PRINCE JAMES dunks another soldier.

scene 29. The Royal Geographical Society's Headquarters, designed by Norman Shaw (1874) is in Kensington – I would have preferred rather less spacious accommodation for the bachelor soldier but sounds of the offscreen barracks' life outside convey the right atmosphere.

RATCLIFFE pours the coffee.

This is the first chance to register Richard's batman, the faithful Ratcliffe, who has been with his boss through thick and thin. Another soldier to whom the army has been everything. It is a totally professional relationship and he is never an accomplice to Richard's malevolence. So, Ratcliffe does not witness here the destruction of the royal pardon which was intended to release Clarence from The Tower.

scenes 30 and 34 were filmed at Royal Woolwich Arsenal in south-east London which is now abandoned by the Army and houses a collection of books from the British Library. Our budget limited us to hiring only one horse, rather than thirty! And so scene 32 was deleted.

29 INT. RICHARD'S SITTING-ROOM – THE BARRACKS – DAY

RATCLIFFE has lit the coal fire, burning merrily in the grate. The little table is laid for English breakfast for two.

RICHARD sits and, as RATCLIFFE pours the coffee, opens a letter with the recognisable Royal Seal that lies next to *The Times* newspaper.

RICHARD reads, lights a cigarette and impassively burns CLARENCE's Royal Pardon. He massages comfort into his aching, withered left hand.

> RICHARD
> (to CAMERA)
> **Clarence still breathes.**
> **Edward still lives and reigns.**
> **When they are gone, then shall I count my**
> **gains.**

Outside, a DRILL-SERGEANT barks orders to his troops.

30 EXT. PARADE GROUND – THE BARRACKS

RICHARD and RATCLIFFE stride briskly past the PLATOON being exercised by the DRILL-SERGEANT, who salutes as the Commander-in-Chief goes by.

31 DELETED

32 INT. DRESSAGE HALL – THE BARRACKS – DAY

30 unharnessed HORSES are being exercised by their GROOMS, trotting and walking round the sawdust oval. RICHARD seems to know each of them, man and beast.

scene 34. Richard III's heraldic device was the boar, a dangerously unpredictable beast, although our ornamental version seemed happy to crunch all day long on slices of Granny Smith.

'James Tyrell – and your most obedient servant.'

All the actors were constantly encouraging to me about the film and some of them about my performance. Adrian Dunbar went further: between takes he was always ready to discuss our scenes. His most telling insight was that an actor, when filming, does not need, as in the theatre, to end a scene with some definite punctuation, the most obvious and necessary of which is to leave the stage. In film, it is the director who decides how each scene will develop into the next. The actors, even when their dialogue is finished, should always be in some transition of thought or emotion.

'Prove me, my gracious Lord.' I was waiting for RL to call out 'Cut' and for the scene to end, when Adrian passed me the next apple which he had been ready to throw at the boar. With some venom, I chucked it at the animal, whose squeal fortuitously provided RL with his transitional cutting point.

96

33   **DELETED**

34   **INT. STABLES – THE BARRACKS – DAY**

There are more immaculately groomed horses in their stalls.
RICHARD pets a couple as he strides along. Then he
notices CORPORAL JAMES TYRELL preparing feed for
the regimental mascot, a huge BOAR. He grinds the mash in
a machine and pours it into the pig-trough.

>   RICHARD
>   (to RATCLIFFE)
>   **What is his name?**

>   RATCLIFFE
>   **His name is Tyrell, sir.**

>   RICHARD
>   **I partly know the man.**

RICHARD joins TYRELL at the BOAR's pen. He watches
the animal scoffing the sticky sludge.

>   RICHARD
>   **Is your name Tyrell?**

>   TYRELL
>   **James Tyrell – and your most obedient servant.**

>   RICHARD
>   **Are you indeed?**

>   TYRELL
>   **Prove me, my gracious Lord.**

The ever-discreet RATCLIFFE does not hear what
RICHARD says next to TYRELL.

scene 35. The Tower of the film is a prison and a fortress. The real Tower of London is the most visited building in Europe. It is very photogenic. When we asked to film there, The Governor of The Tower, not wanting any disruption of life within his fortressed village, advised us to go to Dover Castle, where we would be less hampered by residents and tourists. RL wanted a Lublianka not a tourist attraction. The exterior of our Tower is the formidable Bankside Power Station just along from the archaeological remains of the Rose and Globe theatres where Shakespeare worked. Next door is the newly built, riverside Globe, now ready for productions within the ersatz Elizabethan playhouse.

scene 36. The interior of our Tower was shot in the basement of London County Hall designed by Ralph Knott (1922) on the Thames opposite the Houses of Parliament. This was the headquarters of the Greater London Council until it was disbanded in the 1980s. During filming, County Hall was being converted into an hotel and luxury apartments, although the noise of re-building did not penetrate the cellar.

'O, I have passed a miserable night.' Clarence's renowned speech needed an actor at ease with blank verse, who could avoid presenting it as if it were detached from the rest of the screenplay. Nigel Hawthorne is exemplary: his delivery is sympathetic to the rhythms, through which he finds a genuine melancholy and horror and without which the speech could have seemed nothing more than a Shakespeare golden-oldie.

scene 37. This seems to me the most astonishing of all our locations, perhaps because I did not visit it. The circular slab of concrete ringed with sluggish water is the centre of a disused gasometer.

35 INT. CLARENCE'S CELL – THE TOWER – DAY

The screen is black. A key turns in a lock, a heavy door groans. The click of a switch. CLARENCE stands blinking as the blackness of his concrete cell is turned to savage day by the harsh lights overhead.

36 INT. UNDERGROUND CORRIDOR – THE TOWER – DAY

CLARENCE is lead by his JAILER down an endless echoing tunnel.

> CLARENCE
> **O, I have passed a miserable night.**
> **I thought that I had broken from The Tower**
> **And was embarked to cross to Burgundy:**
> **And, in my company, my brother Richard,**
> **Who from my cabin tempted me to walk**
> **Upon the hatches. As we paced along,**
> **I thought that Richard stumbled and, in falling,**
> **Struck me overboard,**
> **Into the tumbling billows of the main.**

37 EXT. EXERCISE YARD – THE TOWER – DAY

Looking down into a deep windowless shaft. A steel door in one wall opens and CLARENCE is led out by his JAILER.

CLARENCE looks up beyond the bleak, blackened, brick walls to a patch of tumbling cloud.

There are three nightmares in the film – Richard's is actually staged by Shakespeare, Stanley's and Clarence's are both recollected.

Clarence's dream foresees what will soon occur – his death by drowning. It gains force because the audience knows that Richard intends his brother no good.

scene 38. Shakespeare's two murderers are not named, but the businesslike dialogue suggests an officer briefing his men: cf. *Macbeth* (3.2) where another military leader persuades two reluctant subordinates to obey.

CLARENCE

O Lord, I thought what pain it was to drown!
What dreadful noise of water in my ears!
What sights of ugly death within my eyes!
I thought I saw a thousand fearful wrecks,
A thousand men that fishes gnawed upon,
Wedges of gold, great anchors, heaps of pearl,
Inestimable stones, unvalued jewels –
All scattered in the bottom of the sea.

There is a crash of thunder and it begins to rain: big, fat
leaden drops that seem to burst in slow motion on the dusty
ground. The JAILER is transfixed by CLARENCE's dream.

CLARENCE
(continuing)

Some lay in dead men's skulls: and in the holes
Where eyes did once inhabit, there were crept –
As it were in scorn of eyes – reflecting gems,
That wooed the slimy bottom of the deep
And mocked the dead bones that lay
    scattered by.
My dream was lengthened after life.
O, then began the tempest to my soul.
With that, I thought a legion of foul fiends
Environed me and howled in my ears
Such hideous cries that, with the very noise,
I trembling waked and for a season after
Could not believe but that I was in Hell,
Such terrible impression made my dream.

38   EXT. KING'S CROSS – DAY

RATCLIFFE opens the door for RICHARD to emerge
from his car into the quiet back street. No-one is about.

This location in Cheney Road is to one side of King's Cross Station and has often been used in films needing a corner of bygone London. The skeletons of old gasometers in the background are now preserved as examples of Victorian engineering. Two alleyways link Cheney Road to the main road. One of these (just offscreen) is called 'Clarence Passage'; another, 'Stanley Passage'. RL changed the location for the meeting with Tyrell and the NCO.

On the roof of the nineteenth-century flats there, television aerials were temporarily removed or hidden by drying laundry and a pigeon-loft was mocked-up. The day before shooting, I suggested that we see the NCO's wife bringing up refreshments to welcome the distinguished visitor. Josie Kidd, with whom I first acted over thirty years ago in the repertory company at Ipswich, gamely agreed to film only twelve hours after I called her.

'I have it here about me.' This was a chance to show Richard's practised dexterity with his one functioning hand, as he smartly delivers the death warrant and first cash instalment of the murderers' reward.

RICHARD spies TYRELL and a heavyweight NON-COMMISSIONED OFFICER discreetly waiting in the shade of the alley.

As they meet, RATCLIFFE stands apart.

> RICHARD
> **Now then, my hardy, stout-resolved mates;**
> **Are you now going to dispatch this thing?**

> TYRELL
> **We are, my Lord: and need the warrant**
> **That we may be admitted where he is.**

> RICHARD
> (handing over the warrant and a couple of
> banknotes from a stuffed wallet – more money
> later)
> **Well thought upon it. I have it here about me.**
> **Be sudden in the execution,**
> **For Clarence is well-spoken and, perhaps,**
> **May move your hearts to pity.**

> TYRELL
> **We go to use our hands and not our tongues.**

> RICHARD
> **I like you lads. About your business straight.**

The NCO and TYRELL come automatically to attention.

> RICHARD
> (continuing)
> **Your eyes drop millstones, when fools' eyes**
> **fall tears.**

'Clarence has not another day to live.' It was a race to complete this scene before dusk. I spoke these lines just as the sun fell below the horizon of roofs and chimneys.

scene 39. There is a character missing here – Queen Margaret who was Lady Anne's mother-in-law and enemy to practically everybody else. In compensation, I added to the scene Lady Anne, who enters on Richard's arm as if they are now betrothed. Richard has secured an attractive consort, with royal connections, to accompany him through his new civilian life. We begin to chart her decline, as she silently watches her man go about his business.

RICHARD consults his Rolex, massages his left hand and glances at the CAMERA as he gets up to leave.

>   RICHARD
>   (to CAMERA)
> **Clarence has not another day to live.**
> **Which done, God take King Edward to his**
>   **mercy –**
> **And leave the world for me to bustle in.**

39   **INT. PRIVATE DINING-ROOM – THE PALACE –
      NIGHT**

The walls are hung with medieval hunting tapestries and large oil paintings of previous royal occupants. The dining table is spread with lace, damask, gold-plate, fresh flowers and flaming candelabra.

The confident HASTINGS and LADY HASTINGS, the 'deep-revolving, witty' BUCKINGHAM, the apprehensive, good LORD STANLEY with his matronly wife LADY STANLEY and the gaitered ARCHBISHOP, all in full evening-dress, await the entrance of the royal hostess.

A FOOTMAN opens the door for QUEEN ELIZABETH, who glides in, ultra-modishly dressed, on RIVERS' arm. PRINCESS ELIZABETH has been made to come along too.

QUEEN ELIZABETH offers her hand to HASTINGS.

>   HASTINGS
>   (bowing)
> **God make Your Majesty joyful as you**
>   **have been.**

This is an unfortunate reference to current problems.

'Good time of day unto Your Majesty.'

We dine here in the Banqueting Room of the Royal Pavilion in Brighton. It was the first time that a film had been permitted to shoot in the fantastical retreat which the Prince Regent built for weekend rendezvous by the sea. Redecorated in a grand Oriental design by John Nash in 1812, it pre-dates the Victorian Gothic which elsewhere characterises the royal world. Filming was only possible at night-time, once the Pavilion had been closed to its daily paying tourists.

QUEEN ELIZABETH
(sourly, under her breath)
Prime Minister.
This will not be a merry gathering.

QUEEN ELIZABETH greets BUCKINGHAM warmly – a
man whom everyone respects and trusts.

BUCKINGHAM
(kissing the royal hand)
Good time of day unto Your Majesty.

RIVERS
(to LORD STANLEY)
Saw you the King today?

LORD STANLEY
(nervously)
**But now the Duke of Buckingham and I
Are come from visiting His Majesty.**

QUEEN ELIZABETH
(surprised to BUCKINGHAM)
Did you confer with him?

BUCKINGHAM
**Ma'am we did. He desires to make
reconciliation between
Richard Gloucester and your brother here.**

QUEEN ELIZABETH
**Would all were well! But that will never be.
I fear our happiness is at the height.**

As they all look for their places at table, RICHARD bursts
in, immaculate and apparently furious. LADY ANNE is with

She is wearing an evening-gown . . . All Annette Bening's gowns were original 1930s models.

him, feeling out of place. She is wearing an evening-gown of
scarlet – her husband's favourite colour.

> RICHARD
> **Who is it that complains unto the King,**
> **That I, in truth, am stern and love them not?**

RICHARD bows into the silence.

> RICHARD
> (continuing)
> **Because I cannot flatter and speak fair,**
> **I must be held a rancorous enemy.**
> **Cannot a plain man live and think no harm?**

> RIVERS
> **To whom in all this presence speaks your**
> **Grace?**

> RICHARD
> **To you, who've neither honesty nor grace!**
> **When have I injured you?**
> (he sounds so bewildered)
> **When done you wrong?**

> QUEEN ELIZABETH
> (sitting at the head of the table)
> **Come, come, we know your meaning, brother**
> **Gloucester.**

> RICHARD
> **I cannot tell. The world is grown so bad,**
> **That wrens make prey where eagles may**
> **not perch.**

'My brother Clarence is imprisoned by your means.' Why Queen Elizabeth might be accused of antagonism toward Clarence is lost in the mist of the Wars of the Roses. Richard's motive is more clear: his ambition could be impeded by his older brother Clarence who supersedes him in the line to the throne.

'Benedictus . . .' These are not Shakespeare's words but they draw attention away from the principal adversaries to the other diners, as they silently observe the argument.

scene 40. The discussion of Clarence's imprisonment is interrupted to show his murderers arriving at The Tower. In the play, Richard does not hand over the death warrant until after dinner. The long scene which follows (1.4) begins with Clarence's dream and continues right up to his death.

QUEEN ELIZABETH
You envy my advancement and my family.
God grant we never may have need of you.

RICHARD
Meantime, God grants that I have need of *you*.
My brother Clarence is imprisoned by your
means!

QUEEN ELIZABETH
Richard, you do me shameful injury.

Shocked silence all round that such an accusation should be
spoken outloud. The ARCHBISHOP thinks it's time to
say grace.

ARCHBISHOP
Benedictus, benedicat, per Jesum Christum,
Dominum nostrum. Amen.

Most eyes are closed, though BUCKINGHAM takes a peep
at RICHARD.

40 **INT. STAIRWELL – THE TOWER – NIGHT**

BRACKENBURY looks down the steep open stairwell. His
voice echoes as he calls down to the intruding TYRELL and
NCO.

BRACKENBURY
What would you, fellow? And how came
you hither?

TYRELL
I would speak with Clarence; and I came hither
on my legs.

scene 41. Much of the food for this scene was prepared to one side of the Prince Regent's kitchens, where so many royal banquets were cooked and served. Film food is rarely as appetising as it looks on the screen. Our half-lobsters, dressed out of their shells, along with the fresh fruit and salads, all started to decay over the 48 hours we were in the Pavilion. Hour by hour, under the hot lamps, the mayonnaise curdled, the bread curled and rotting fish began to stink. Only the 'wine' (diluted Ribena) was replenished for each take and therefore safe to swallow.

TYRELL insolently holds out CLARENCE's death-warrant to BRACKENBURY, who reluctantly starts down the stairs to read it.

41   **INT. PRIVATE DINING-ROOM – THE PALACE – NIGHT**

The stately HEAD BUTLER and full MALE AND FEMALE STAFF are expertly serving soup and wine. Slurping and breaking of bread. RICHARD manages, as usual, with just one hand.

> QUEEN ELIZABETH
> (breaking the long silence)
> **I never did incense His Majesty**
> **Against your brother Clarence.**

> RICHARD
> **You may deny that you –**

> RIVERS
> **She may, my Lord –**

> RICHARD
> **She may, Earl Rivers! Why who knows not so?**
> **She may do more, sir, than denying that.**
> **She may help you to many great promotions.**
> **What may she *not* ?**

> RIVERS
> **My Lord of Gloucester, I have too long borne**
> **Your blunt upbraidings and your bitter scoffs.**

'Were sympathetic to the enemy.' This is my clarification of the play's 'Were factious to the house of Lancaster.'

'What you have been before and what you are.
Indeed what I have been and what I am.' In the play, this reads:

> What you have been ere this and what you are;
> Withal, what I have been and what I am.

Here and elsewhere, arcaisms have been adjusted so as not to puzzle the modern ear. I am prepared for the accusation of being patronising. When Maggie Smith and I were in *Much Ado About Nothing* for the National Theatre (1966), Robert Graves was credited under Shakespeare in the programme for the synonyms he had substituted for some of the more obscure vocabulary. Graves was lambasted by those drama critics who felt that a crucial part of the experience of seeing and hearing Shakespeare was in measuring up to the difficulties, rather than in side-stepping them. Nevertheless, I have often since clarified Elizabethan texts in performance: e.g., I always say 'instantly' instead of 'presently', whose meaning has reversed itself over the last 400 years. No-one has yet complained. Perhaps it is only an offence to alter Shakespeare if you confess to it.

QUEEN ELIZABETH

I had rather be a country serving-maid,
Than a great Queen in this condition
To be so baited, scorned and stormed at.
By heaven, I will acquaint His Majesty.

RICHARD

Tell him and spare not. Look, what I have said,
I will avouch in presence of the King.
Before you were Queen, yes, or your husband
    King,
I was a packhorse in his great affairs.
In all that time, you and your brother here
Were sympathetic to the enemy.
Let me put in your minds, if you forget,
What you have been before and what you are.
Indeed what I have been and what I am.

QUEEN ELIZABETH
(to herself)
A bottled spider.
(sweetly)
My dear brother-in-law, in those busy days
When now you try to prove us enemies,
We followed then Edward, our lawful King.

RIVERS
So should she you, if you should be her King.

RICHARD
If I should be? I'd rather be a pedlar.
I am too childish-foolish for this world.

Once all the dialogue was filmed, there was scarcely time for the all-important reaction shots from the other guests at dinner. This would involve moving the camera to Queen Elizabeth's point of view, with the attendant lighting change to illuminate the wall opposite her. Dawn was breaking and so instead of moving the camera and lights, we moved the actors, who exchanged places with those opposite. The wall behind Queen Elizabeth thus did double service.

QUEEN ELIZABETH
(exploding)
You poisonous, bunch–backed toad!

The company has listened to this bitter exchange and been impressed by RICHARD's cool righteousness. Certainly QUEEN ELIZABETH has now gone too far.

BUCKINGHAM
(leans in to QUEEN ELIZABETH)
Have done! Have done.

QUEEN ELIZABETH
(crying now, to RIVERS)
Small joy have I in being this country's Queen.
(*sotto voce*)
Oh, Buckingham, take heed of yonder dog!
Look, when he fawns, he bites.
CATESBY enters discreetly. All turn to the King's private secretary.

CATESBY
(bowing)
Your Majesty, His Majesty has called for you.

QUEEN ELIZABETH rises and takes PRINCESS ELIZABETH out with her. RIVERS follows her swiftly. CATESBY wonders what he has interrupted but also withdraws.

The guests who have risen and bowed are not sure what they should do next. Pity to waste a free banquet. RICHARD is relaxed.

'Nothing that I respect, my gracious Lord.'

Richard's aim is to increase suspicion of the foreigners, Queen Elizabeth and Rivers, thereby drawing Buckingham, Hastings, Stanley and the Archbishop into his circle. In this and similar two-shots, I was able to reduce my height a little, by bending my knees out of view of the camera. Richard's deformed spine would have foreshortened his upper body. In long shot, this was not of course practical: but I like it best when Richard is shorter than I am.

'I do the wrong. . .' These two lines were cut in the editing-room, so that the scene now ends with Richard's confidential glance to camera in reaction to the Archbishop's piety.

'A virtuous and a Christian-like conclusion . . .' Rivers was robbed of these lines, in order to introduce the Archbishop.

In the play, there are three bishops – all Catholic, one of them a Cardinal. Our Archbishop is head of the Protestant Established Church and at the centre of the power- brokers' set, a politician ambitious for the survival and promotion of his Church.

The Archbishop plays a dangerous game in encouraging Richmond to take up armed revolt, long before others decide that Richard has to be dealt with. To look at, butter wouldn't melt in Roger Hammond's mouth.

RICHARD
What did she say, my Lord of Buckingham?

BUCKINGHAM
(quietly, to RICHARD)
Nothing that I respect, my gracious Lord.

RICHARD takes his place and the others follow suit. They look toward him and he smiles innocently back at them. He begins to eat. They all do the same.

RICHARD
I cannot blame her, by God's Holy Mother.
(turning to CAMERA and not overheard)
I do the wrong and first begin to brawl.
And seem a saint when most I play the devil.

ARCHBISHOP
A virtuous and a Christian-like conclusion,
To pray for those who have done wrong to you.

RICHARD smiles his thanks for that supportive remark. The banquet proceeds uneasily.

42 **INT. CORRIDOR OUTSIDE PRISON BATH-HOUSE – THE TOWER – NIGHT**

TYRELL and the NCO peer through a windowed door and see their victim at his ablutions in the communal bath-house.

TYRELL
What! Are you afraid?

NCO
Not to kill him, having a warrant for it; but to

scene 42. This truncated version of one of the few prose scenes is an example of Shakespeare presenting ordinary citizens caught up in the state affairs of the principal characters. The NCO's venality is a chilling reminder that, under tyranny, obeying orders often takes precedence over doing what is right.

In the play, there are a few other glimpses of the world beyond the corridors of power. Three citizens discuss politics (2.3) and in a solo sonnet, the Scrivener confides to the audience his knowledge of Richard's manipulation of public relations (3.6).

'I had forgot the reward.'
Michael Elphick (NCO) and I met backstage, working at the Chichester Festival Theatre in 1966. He was a drama student, filling in as a stage-hand during his long vacation. I was on stage with Laurence Olivier's National Theatre Company, which used to vacate its home at the Old Vic Theatre in London to present a summer repertoire in the Sussex countryside.

'reading a Bible.' At the RNT, Richard had given his own battle-worn Bible to Clarence to comfort him in his imprisonment. It foreshadowed Richard playing the holy man in his duping of the Lord Mayor and city gentlemen. Having omitted this Bible-business in scene 21, a newspaper replaces it as Clarence's reading-matter.

be damned for killing him, from which no warrant can defend me.

TYRELL
I thought you had been resolute.

NCO
So I am – to let him live.

TYRELL
I'll back to Richard Gloucester and tell him so.

NCO
No. Stay a little. Some certain dregs of conscience are yet within me.

TYRELL
Remember our reward, when the deed's done.

NCO
Phew! He dies. I had forgot the reward.

TYRELL
Where's your conscience now?

NCO
In the Duke of Gloucester's purse.

43   INT. PRISON BATH-HOUSE – THE TOWER –
     NIGHT

TYRELL and the NCO enter and approach CLARENCE as he lies in a long, enamelled bath, reading a Bible.

CLARENCE
In God's name, what are you?

Nigel Hawthorne followed *Richard III* with more Shakespeare – playing Malvolio in Trevor Nunn's film of *Twelfth Night*.

NCO
A man as you are.

CLARENCE
But not, as I am, royal.

NCO
Nor you, as we are, loyal.

CLARENCE
Who sent you to me? And why have you come?

NCO
To . . . to . . . to –

CLARENCE
– murder me!

TYRELL & NCO
Ay, ay.

CLARENCE
But how, my friends, have I offended you?

NCO
Offended us you have not – but King Edward.

CLARENCE
I will send you to my brother Richard,
Who shall reward you better for my life
Than will the King for tidings of my death.

NCO
You are deceived. Your brother Richard
hates you.

'O do not slander him, for he is kind.' To the end, Clarence is blind to Richard's infidelity. Just as he might begin to realise the significance of his nightmare about drowning, he is thrust into the bath water. In the play, the first murderer stabs Clarence:

> Take that and that. If all this will not do.
> I'll drown you in the malmsey-butt within. (1.4.268)

scene 44. Richard's preoccupation with Clarence's death is an appropriate moment to indicate that his marriage to Lady Anne is already turning sour.

When the final screenplay was issued, it was called 'the Bible' and almost as much revered, in that every department took even the most casual of instructions as a rule of law. For instance, just because I had written that Richard wore a Rolex watch, the property department hired a genuine, vintage timepiece, worth £5,000, for me to wear onscreen.

CLARENCE
O no! He loves me and he holds me dear.
Go you to him, tell him and he will weep.

TYRELL
Yes, millstones! As he lessoned us to weep.

CLARENCE
O do not slander him, for he is kind.

TYRELL
Right; as snow in harvest.

The NCO efficiently holds down CLARENCE, as
TYRELL slices open his throat and then pushes the dying
man's head under the water. A rush of red billows through
the water toward the CAMERA.

44   **INT. RICHARD'S APARTMENT – THE**
     BARRACKS – NIGHT

RICHARD, smoking, in his favourite armchair. He is
rubbing his painful, left hand. There is a quiet knock at
the door.

RICHARD
Ratcliffe?

RATCLIFFE enters and hands over a small packet.
RICHARD nods. RATCLIFFE leaves. RICHARD
unwraps the packet, which contains CLARENCE's cracked
spectacles. RICHARD downs his glass of whisky.

RICHARD ignores his bride, LADY ANNE, alluringly half-
naked in her red lingerie, at their bedroom door. He checks
his Rolex and bustles past her, closing the bedroom door
behind him. LADY ANNE is alone once more.

scene 46. Another silent, pictorial presentation of a barren relationship. Richard and Anne do not speak, not just because I invented the scene, but because they have nothing to say to each other. She takes a pill: he an Abdulla. The biggest surprise when looking at photos and film of the 1930s is the amount of smoking that was fashionable. The smokers in the film, apart from Richard, are Lady Anne, Buckingham, Catesby, King Edward, Queen Elizabeth, the NCO, Ratcliffe, Rivers, Stanley, Tyrell and as many of the extras who cared to.

45   EXT. SOUTH-COAST SHORELINE ROAD – DAY

The sun glints on the grey sea of the Channel and on the
gleaming bodywork of RICHARD's car, preceded by its
escort. Seagulls.

46   INT. RICHARD'S CAR – DAY

RATCLIFFE drives. Behind are RICHARD and LADY
ANNE, she, got up for a royal garden party and looking
perfectly composed, yet perfectly unhappy, in her wide-
brimmed hat. She swallows a couple of tranquillizers with
iced water in a crystal tumbler.

RICHARD, in summer linen and a panama, ignores her.

47   EXT. SUMMER HOUSE – COUNTRY RETREAT –
DAY

KING EDWARD and his COURTIERS are hoping a dose
of sea air will halt his physical decline.

The large cast-iron summer-house, looking out to sea, has
every convenience. There are wicker chairs with comfily
padded cushions and tables have the remains of afternoon tea
and cucumber sandwiches.

PRINCE JAMES is playing with his pedal-car, while his
NANNY looks on.

KING EDWARD in his wheelchair is wrapped in plaid
blankets. He is flushed with his efforts to bring old
antagonists into agreement, so as to bolster his wife's
powerbase. Participating are QUEEN ELIZABETH and
RIVERS, HASTINGS and BUCKINGHAM.

'now have I done a good day's work.' This is another reference to events which have happened before the film's story begins. We had to hope that the audience would not want to enquire into the details of the disagreement which King Edward has now patched-up into 'this united league'. The main point is simple – that the King has strengthened his own power-base, in the hope that it might survive him to support Queen Elizabeth and the succession of their eldest son.

KING EDWARD
Why so; now have I done a good day's work.
Now friends, continue this united league.
Rivers and Hastings, take each other's hand.

RIVERS
Hastings, my soul is purged from grudging
    hate.

HASTINGS
Your Majesty, I truly swear the like!

KING EDWARD
Elizabeth, you are not exempt in this.
Wife, greet Lord Hastings. Let him kiss
    your hand.

QUEEN ELIZABETH
(graciously proffering her gloved hand to the
Prime Minister)
There, Hastings.

HASTINGS kisses the QUEEN's hand.

KING EDWARD
Now, princely Buckingham,
    (laughter)
Make me happy in this unity.

Everyone looks forward with varying enthusiasm to one of
BUCKINGHAM's elegant speeches.

We wanted to show the sickly King Edward recuperating away from city life. The Esplanade of the De la Warr Pavilion at Bexhill-on-Sea was designed by Mendelsohn and Chermayeff (1935).

With doctor and nurse in attendance, the royal courtiers have joined the King as he takes the sunshine – lasting evidence of England's hottest summer for two centuries. High above the English Channel, the warm offshore breezes are a little too evident, as they billow frocks and threaten to blow away wide-brimmed hats.

This was a difficult location to shoot. The scene had to be shot rather flatly across a diagonal of 180 degrees to avoid seeing the hotels and fripperies of modern Bexhill which lay behind the camera, as it faces out to sea. The cupolas on the terrace were temporary additions from the art department.

BUCKINGHAM
(to the QUEEN)
Whenever Buckingham does turn his hate
Upon Your Majesty, God punish me
With hate from those where I expect most love.
When I have most need to employ a friend,
And most assured that he is a friend –

KING EDWARD
(interrupting, as he sees RICHARD and LADY
ANNE approaching)
Richard!

The newly-weds look straight out of *Vogue*. LADY ANNE
links her arm through RICHARD's useless one. He needs
his other for the cane. He breaks from his wife and strides
forward to his brother. He bows to the KING and QUEEN.

RICHARD
Good morning to my sovereign King –
and Queen.

KING EDWARD
Now, Richard, we have done a good
day's work:
Made peace of enmity, fair love of hate.

RICHARD
It's death to me to be at enmity:
I hate it and desire all good men's love.
(with absolute commitment; to the QUEEN)
First, Madam, I entreat true peace of you,
Which I will purchase with my duteous service.

Kristin Scott Thomas sheltering from the wind and the sun. Only those who bring their own chairs and the actors who are obligingly provided with them by the props department have anywhere to sit between filming. Often one's own chair is occupied.

PRINCESS ELIZABETH. In the play she remains offstage. Having introduced her into the film, here is an ironic moment preparing for scene 101, when Richard hopes to marry her.

'Who knows not that the gentle Duke is dead?' Here is an odd acting problem – why, if he is upset by Clarence's death, does Richard allow himself to be so jolly up to this point in the scene? Perhaps because a courtier is duty-bound to reflect the monarch's disposition. King Edward is in celebratory mood, so, therefore, is the ever-polite Richard.

RICHARD goes round the gathering to each in turn, shaking hands, patting elbows, slapping backs.

>   RICHARD
>   (continuing)
>   **Of you, my noble, dear Lord Buckingham,**
>   (smiling broadly)
>   **If ever any grudge were lodged between us!**
>   **Of you, Lord Hastings – and you, dear Rivers –**
>   **Who, all without desert, have frowned on me –**
>   **Indeed, of all!**

RICHARD charmingly kisses PRINCESS ELIZABETH, who ever-so-slightly recoils. Sycophantic approval all round. LADY ANNE feels left out.

>   RICHARD
>   (continuing; to the King)
>   **I do not know that Englishman alive,**
>   **With whom my soul is any jot at odds**
>   **More than the infant that is born tonight.**
>   (aside to CAMERA)
>   **I thank my God, for my humility.**

General relief and approval of this reconciliation.

>   QUEEN ELIZABETH
>   **I wish to God all strifes were settled so.**
>   **My sovereign Lord, I do beseech Your Majesty**
>   **To bring your brother Clarence to Your Grace.**

>   RICHARD
>   **Why, Madam, have I offered love for this?**
>   **Who knows not that the gentle Duke is dead?**

There is near-panic. Scene 47 ends with a reverse-shot, to complete the other 180 degrees and to reveal the exterior of Brighton Pavilion, which in reality is thirty or so miles away along the coast from Bexhill. At the end of two long nights of filming, for scenes 39, 41, 48, 49, 50, the final shot was just fitted in, as the early-morning sun lit up the Pavilion's rear elevation.

General consternation and disbelief.

> KING EDWARD
> **'Who knows not he is dead?' Who knows he is?**

Exchange of worried looks.

> QUEEN ELIZABETH
> **All-seeing Heaven, what a world is this!**

> KING EDWARD
> (continuing; to CATESBY)
> **Is Clarence dead? The order was reversed.**

CATESBY looks bewildered.

> RICHARD
> (whispering to KING EDWARD)
> **But he, poor man, by your first order died**
> **And that a winged Mercury did bear.**
> **Some tardy cripple bore the countermand.**

> KING EDWARD
> (stammers, beginning a severe asthma attack)
> **O God! I fear Thy justice will take hold**
> **Of me and mine – and mine – and yours**
> **   for this.**
> **Rivers help me to my bed. O, poor Clarence.**

There is near-panic. The NURSE and DOCTOR take professional control and wheel the ailing KING EDWARD back towards the house.

QUEEN ELIZABETH, PRINCESS ELIZABETH and RIVERS chase after KING EDWARD's wheelchair, up toward the house.

scene 48 was filmed in the Long Gallery on the ground floor of the Brighton Pavilion.

Richard can hardly wait for the fortuitous death of his elder brother and the power vacuum that his own Lord Protectorship can fill. Buckingham is already at his side, as Richard slides over to Hastings and Catesby whose support, as Prime Minister and Civil Service Chief, he will also need. Lady Anne is ignored once more.

All the scenes at Brighton Pavilion (39, 41, 48, 49 and 50) were shot through the night. The day before night-filming is for sleep, which I can usually induce, with the aid of Boots' waxen ear-plugs and a British Airways' eye-shade. During the working night, as the real world outside sleeps, the enclosed fraternity of film-making intensifies. Caffeine is on tap from the tea and coffee urns, although I enjoy cat-napping whether sitting, leaning or lying down.

After the hot meal in the early hours, I restored energies by sleeping on my caravan fold-down double-bed, my right cheek on the pillow, careful to avoid disturbing Daniel Parker's prosthetics on my left side. The night's work over, there was breakfast at dawn and then a second day's sleep at the hotel, with ear-plugs again, muffling the chambermaids at their housekeeping.

'This news is bad indeed.' This line and Richard's reply are borrowed from elsewhere in the play (1.1) where Hastings has been newly released from The Tower – a sub-plot that was omitted because of its long roots in the Wars of the Roses.

48 **INT. DRAWING-ROOM – COUNTRY RETREAT – DAY**

Everyone is waiting for the outcome of KING EDWARD's attack.

The super-cool RICHARD takes out an Abdulla. At his side, BUCKINGHAM offers a light and then lights his own fat cigar – he is smooth as an agent and RICHARD is soon to become his star client.

> RICHARD
> (aside to BUCKINGHAM)
> **This is the fruits of rashness.**
> (to HASTINGS and CATESBY)
> **Marked you not,**
> **How that the guilty brother of the Queen**
> **Looked pale, when he did hear of Clarence's**
> **death?**
> **God will revenge it!**

The door opens. The DUCHESS OF YORK has arrived with LORD STANLEY. BUCKINGHAM goes to greet her.

> DUCHESS OF YORK
> **O Clarence, Clarence, my unhappy son.**

> LORD STANLEY
> **This news is bad indeed. What, is he in his bed?**

> RICHARD
> **He is. O he has over-used his royal person**
> **much.**

scene 49. RL contained all this action within a single static shot from the point of view of the dying King. As his breathing stops, Queen Elizabeth leaves, attended by her brother and then by the Archbishop. The doctor's job is over. Princess Elizabeth is left alone. Above her is the magnificent ceiling of the Brighton Pavilion's Music Room, recently restored to glory following its partial destruction in a storm.

Before the DUCHESS OF YORK can be led to her son's bedside, there is a SCREAM and commotion from the floor above.

49   INT. THE KING'S BEDROOM – COUNTRY
      RETREAT – DAY

A scene of mayhem.

On top of the royal bed, KING EDWARD has died, his mouth fixed in an agonised last gasp for breath.

On one side of him, his DOCTOR searches for a pulse with his stethoscope.

On the other, QUEEN ELIZABETH tries to revive her husband's corpse, with thumps of rage and fear. She never planned to be a powerless widow.

As RIVERS tries to restrain her, QUEEN ELIZABETH rushes out, uncontrollable.

RIVERS follows her down the corridor, without a glance at PRINCESS ELIZABETH, who gazes at death for the first time in her protected, young life.

The DOCTOR examines the corpse. The NURSE looks tearful, as she closes the shutters. The ARCHBISHOP mumbles an obsequy.

50   INT. DRAWING-ROOM – COUNTRY RETREAT –
      DAY

QUEEN ELIZABETH rushes down the stairs and collapses onto a chair.

                    DUCHESS OF YORK
        What means this scene of rude impatience?

BUCKINGHAM takes control. The Lord Protector's dry-eyed party is framed together, as they face the grieving mother, widow and her brother.

'We are to reap the harvest of his son.' Buckingham needs no prompt from Richard as he presents his plan. 'The King is dead. Long live the King – and the Lord Protector!' so to speak.

QUEEN ELIZABETH
Edward, my Lord, your son, our King is dead!

Everyone wonders what should happen next. A nervous silence. Before HASTINGS has a chance to speak, BUCKINGHAM takes control.

RICHARD looks to HASTINGS and LORD STANLEY. They nod their approval.

RIVERS enters, out of breath, and goes to help his sister.

QUEEN ELIZABETH
**Why grow the branches, now the root is
    withered?**
Why wither not the leaves, the sap being gone?

DUCHESS OF YORK
Alas! I am the mother of these griefs.
**On me pour all your tears; I am your
    sorrow's nurse.**

RICHARD
Elizabeth, have comfort. All of us have cause
To wail the dimming of our shining star.

BUCKINGHAM
Though we have spent our harvest of this King,
We are to reap the harvest of his son.

RIVERS
Sister, think you like a careful mother
**Of the Prince of Wales, your son. Send straight
    for him.**
Let him be crowned; in him your comfort lies.

'Why "with some little train", my Lord of Buckingham?'
Having been enthralled by Robert Downey Jr's performance as Chaplin, I jumped at the chance to act with him in *Restoration* in the summer of 1994. As the wastrel Merivel, he effortlessly combined innocence with sexiness, sentiment with slapstick. As his loyal servant Will Gates, I found it easy to be both paternal and respectful.

We were under pressure from our financiers who wanted another internationally recognised name in the cast list, as well as Annette Bening. I called Robert at his home in Malibu, knowing that Rivers was too small a part for him to accept. I misjudged his generosity. He wanted to help the film be made and immediately cleared his diary for three weeks in London. *Richard III* and *Restoration* were released in North America on the same day, 22 December 1995.

'And so in me.' Rivers, the American playboy, does not have a chance against the scheming heavyweight team of Richard and Buckingham.

Defers to Hastings. My back to camera, it was possible to identify Hastings by adding 'Prime Minister?' onto the final soundtrack.

BUCKINGHAM
(to QUEEN ELIZABETH)
Meseemeth good that, with some little train,
The Prince be brought to London to be
    crowned.

RIVERS
Why 'with some little train', my Lord of
    Buckingham?

BUCKINGHAM
Lest by a multitude, dear sir,
The new-healed wound of civil war break out.

RICHARD
(supporting BUCKINGHAM)
I hope the King made peace with all of us:
And the compact is firm and true in me.

RIVERS
(reluctantly)
And so in me. And so, I think, in all.
Therefore, I say, with noble Buckingham,
It's fitting that so few should meet the Prince.

Everyone nods agreement and looks toward RICHARD, the
Lord Protector, who, in turn, defers to HASTINGS, the
Prime Minister.

HASTINGS
And so say I.

RICHARD
Then, be it so.

DUCHESS OF YORK. I had always hoped that Maggie Smith would agree to play my mother, a small part for which she is, of course, far too young, but which needs a dominant personality to convey the emotional barrenness of Richard's childhood.

Maggie and I first made contact in 1964, when she was a young star of Laurence Olivier's newly formed National Theatre Company. She was about to play Beatrice in Franco Zeffirelli's production of *Much Ado About Nothing*. The search was on for a young Claudio, a part I had played three years before, in my first job at the Belgrade Theatre, Coventry. Having seen me in my West End début in *A Scent of Flowers*, Maggie recommended me to Olivier and Zeffirelli. I auditioned in front of all the National Theatre directors and joined the company to play Claudio again.

Also gathered beneath Olivier's wing were many young actors hoping for the same roles – Jeremy Brett, Mike Gambon, Edward Hardwicke, Anthony Hopkins, Derek Jacobi, Edward Petherbridge, Ronald Pickup, John Stride, Christopher Timothy and Michael York as well as the established younger stars like Colin Blakely, Albert Finney, Frank Finlay and Robert Stephens. Eight months later, I left the company and although Olivier wrote to me that I should stay to build up my personal repertoire with him and that he was 'haunted by the spectre of lost opportunity', I found I could get better parts as a freelance actor.

I did not work with Dame Maggie again until the film. I see everything she appears in, but missed her stage début in Oxford as Viola in *Twelfth Night* (1952) and her later Shakespeare during her 1976-80 sojourn in Stratford, Ontario, where she played Queen Elizabeth to Brian Bedford's Richard III.

RIVERS leads QUEEN ELIZABETH toward the door,
where the ARCHBISHOP is waiting with professional
commiseration. They leave.

> DUCHESS OF YORK
> (following)
> **Now two mirrors of my husband's likeness**
> **Are cracked in pieces, by malignant death.**
> (to LORD STANLEY, who offers his arm)
> **And I, for comfort, have but one false glass,**
> **That grieves me when I see my shame in him.**

> RICHARD
> **Madam, Mother, I do humbly crave**
> **your blessing.**

> DUCHESS OF YORK
> (sourly)
> **God bless you – and put meakness in**
> **your breast,**
> **Love, charity, obedience and true duty!**

The DUCHESS OF YORK sails out with LORD
STANLEY.

HASTINGS and CATESBY see RICHARD is upset and
discreetly leave.

> RICHARD
> (wryly; but he's been hurt by his mother)
> **Amen! And make me die a good old man.**
> **That is the butt-end of a mother's blessing.**
> **I marvel that Her Grace did leave it out!**

scene 51. We used the exterior of the London County Hall in whose basement Clarence was killed.

RICHARD and BUCKINGHAM walk through the imposing lobby.
The film's architecture radically changes with this expression of the Lord Protector's power, the lobby of the Senate House in London University (built in 1936) with its large expanses of marble. During the Second World War, the Ministry of Information occupied the Senate House, from which was broadcast information about Dunkirk and the D-Day landings.

It took five days to add the atmospheric footsteps to the finished soundtrack. To facilitate this and to prevent the actors' actual footsteps competing with their dialogue, any leather soles were cushioned during filming, by applied strips of thin foam-rubber.

146

> BUCKINGHAM
> (taking RICHARD's arm)
> **My Lord Protector.**

Agent and client have made a contract. They leave,
forgetting LADY ANNE.

A FOOTMAN respectfully draws the blinds.

51   **EXT. LORD PROTECTOR'S HEADQUARTERS –
     DAY**

RATCLIFFE manoeuvres the Lord Protector's limousine,
carrying RICHARD and BUCKINGHAM, through the tall,
wrought-iron gates into an enclosed courtyard.

52   **INT. LOBBY – LORD PROTECTOR'S
     HEADQUARTERS – DAY**

RICHARD and BUCKINGHAM walk through the
imposing lobby.

53   **INT. HALL/STAIRWAY – LORD PROTECTOR'S
     HEADQUARTERS – DAY**

RICHARD and BUCKINGHAM walk through the hall
and up the grand staircase.

> BUCKINGHAM
> **My Lord, whoever journeys to the Prince,**
> **For God's sake, let not us two stay at home.**
> **And let us part Earl Rivers from the Prince.**

scene 54. Although we filmed Richard's point of view at the door of his magnificent new, empty office, its splendour had been pre-empted by scenes 52 and 53 in the public lobby. In deleting the scene, the last two lines of the previous scene had to go as well. This was unfortunate. 'I as a child, will go by your direction' is an ironic, yet heartfelt, reference to the Duchess of York's lines in scene 50.

The oil painting is now revealed later, in scene 74, by which time it is appropriate that Richard's self-confidence should be increasingly on display.

scenes 55 & 56 were shot inside the Pearl Assurance Building.

The AIR HOSTESS, whom I always imagined might have been crowned 'Miss Pan Am 1935', is identified by her hat. In the background, the bedroom door silently opens to admit Tyrell.

An early draft had Rivers executed by Tyrell in The Tower, his body thrown into the murky, fast-flowing Thames. The more distinctive death of the final screenplay was devised by RL. The nasty stabbing effect was achieved by filming a blade piercing a dummy body and then transferring it via computer onto the film of Robert Downey's torso, which thankfully remains unhurt and unscarred.

RICHARD
My other self.
My oracle, my prophet, my dear Buckingham.
I, as a child, will go by your direction.

54 **INT. LORD PROTECTOR'S OFFICE – DAY**

RICHARD and BUCKINGHAM have reached the door to
the office of the Lord Protector.

RICHARD pushes open the door, revealing the interior of
his newly appointed working premises, worthy of the most
powerful leader in the country and dominated by an iconic
oil painting of a physically perfect RICHARD, which is
mounted on the end wall.

55 **INT. HOTEL CORRIDOR – DAY**

CHAMBERMAID, with towels, notes 'Do not Disturb' sign
on a bedroom door and carries on along the corridor.
TYRELL, approaching from the opposite direction, gives
her a wink.

56 **INT. HOTEL BEDROOM – DAY**

Through the thin curtains, the afternoon sun shines on
RIVERS, lying back, naked, on the brass-headed double-bed
in the luxury hotel room, which he has rented for a couple
of hours. The AIR HOSTESS french-kisses him.

The CAMERA closes in on RIVERS.

As Miss Pan-Am moves down his chest to attend to lower
parts, unseen by him, the door silently opens a little. CLOSE
on RIVERS, as his ecstasy rapidly reaches an agonising
climax, a long, sharp blade slices up through the mattress,
emerging out of his chest.

Train whistle. The housekeeper in Hitchcock's *The Thirty-nine Steps* (1935) discovers a corpse and opens her mouth to scream in time with the whistle of the steam-engine carrying away the supposed murderer, Richard Hannay.

scene 58. I had written for an earlier draft:

> **INT. ROYAL TRAIN – DAY**
>
> A comfortable drawing-room on wheels.
>
> The slim, rather cocky heir to the throne, Edward, PRINCE OF WALES, in his private-school uniform, is taking tea, opposite his massive minder, the Duke of Buckingham, whose cigar smoke lingers in the beams of sunshine.
>
> The Prince of Wales takes a crumpled pack of ten Senior Service from his trouser pocket. The ever-obliging Buckingham offers him a light.

Shortage of funds and time robbed the new young King of this first entrance.

scene 59 was shot on the 5-mile steam locomotive Bluebell Railway in Sussex, which was saved from closure by its Preservation Society in 1955.

scene 60 shows again the Gothic splendour of Strawberry Hill House.

electric toy train is a visual pun on Rivers' 'why with some little train?' (scene 50) and was invented for Bob Crowley's settings at the RNT, when a similar model, with its illuminated carriage windows, chugged across the darkened stage of the Lyttelton Theatre.

'I long with all my heart to see the Prince of Wales.' The teenage Prince has presumably been away at Eton College or some other privileged educational establishment, where young boys are turned into young gentlemen.

The AIR HOSTESS screams simultaneously with a piercing Train whistle.

57 EXT. RAILWAY VIADUCT – DAY

Across the massive monument to Victorian engineering, a steam train thunders forward, pulling its royal carriages through vistas of an idyllic, rural landscape.

58 DELETED

59 EXT. THE COUNTRYSIDE – DAY

The steam train rushes on towards the capital, as the countryside gives way to a cityscape.

60 INT. DRAWING-ROOM – THE PALACE – DAY

There are two sets of double-doors ajar, through which runs the track for PRINCE JAMES's electric toy train. This miniature version of his brother's train buzzes round and round, in and out.

QUEEN ELIZABETH and DUCHESS OF YORK, his doting mater and grandmama, watch him at play. Both are in mourning weeds. By herself, at the window, PRINCESS ELIZABETH still remembers her father's death.

> DUCHESS OF YORK
> **I long with all my heart to see the Prince
> of Wales.**
> **I hope he is much grown since last I saw him.**

> PRINCE JAMES
> **They say my Uncle Richard grew so fast
> That he could gnaw a crust at two hours old.**

'Pitchers have ears.' Today's English audience will misleadingly hear the nonsensical 'pictures have ears'. Americans, like Queen Elizabeth, will understand Shakespeare better. Even household items may be bugged in the Lord Protector's regime. No-one and nothing can be trusted – not even a jug on the tea-table.

GEORGE STANLEY. Lord Stanley's 'young son George' will eventually escape when Richard takes him hostage before the final battle. I had wanted Richard's last and youngest victim to be his most vulnerable, a child who was even more incapacitated. We were unable to find a boy or youth with Down's Syndrome whose guardians would allow him to be filmed.

When I played the mentally handicapped Walter for Stephen Frears (Channel 4: 1981), I had worked with a young man with Down's Syndrome. The two of us were at a carol service in the institution where Walter lived. The keenness with which Peter returned to his starting position as the scene was repeated over and over showed how much he relished being the centre of the camera's attention. One of the hospital nurses was played by Jim Broadbent.

George plays with a model aeroplane, as his father wears the uniform of a senior officer in the Royal Air Force. He is played by Ryan Gilmore, a veteran from commercials.

QUEEN ELIZABETH
A parlous boy. Go to, you are too shrewd.

DUCHESS OF YORK
Elizabeth, be not angry with your son.

QUEEN ELIZABETH
Pitchers have ears.

A KNOCK at the door.

A FOOTMAN lets in LORD STANLEY, holding by the hand his 6-year-old son, GEORGE STANLEY, who has Down's Syndrome. The little boy carries a model plane. With them is HENRY RICHMOND.

PRINCESS ELIZABETH's eyes light up at the sight of her favourite young man.

DUCHESS OF YORK
What news, Lord Stanley?

LORD STANLEY
Such news that grieves me to report.

QUEEN ELIZABETH
(impatiently)
What is your news?

LORD STANLEY
(reluctantly)
Your brother . . . Rivers is murdered.

PRINCE JAMES shows his toy train to GEORGE STANLEY, who laughs as he bombards it with his own model plane.

The rock-like Duchess. Film actors need to relax whilst waiting for the cameras to turn, without losing concentration. Some like to stay in character throughout the day, on and off the set. I was a little bit like that, wanting to hold on to Richard's physique and gait. Some actors retire to their caravans to snooze, or to do a solitary crossword. Others prefer a chat. Whatever, once camera and lights are in place, everyone stops to concentrate on the actors.

When I first filmed, I was embarrassed by all those potential critics who had taken up vantage positions by the camera, until I realised that they were all friends, alertly concerned that everything should look and sound exactly right and thereby contributing helpfully to the concentration of the moment.

scene 61. By now, the very sight of Tyrell is threatening.

> QUEEN ELIZABETH
> (although she knows the answer)
> **By whom?**

LORD STANLEY can't bring himself to reply.

> QUEEN ELIZABETH
> (continuing; to RICHMOND)
> **Richmond?**

> RICHMOND
> (calmly)
> **Richard and Buckingham.**

> QUEEN ELIZABETH
> **I see the ruin of my family.**

> DUCHESS OF YORK
> **Blood against blood; self against self.**
> **Oh, let me die to look on death no more.**

LORD STANLEY attends to the rock-like Duchess.

QUEEN ELIZABETH and PRINCESS ELIZABETH comfort each other's grief.

RICHMOND bends down to play with the uncomprehending GEORGE STANLEY, still waving his model plane over the toy train.

To escape from this aerial attack, PRINCE JAMES crawls after the train, as it goes out through the door.

61   **INT. CORRIDOR – THE PALACE – DAY**

As the train runs over the parquet floor of the corridor, a booted foot halts it along the track. PRINCE JAMES looks up into the smiling face of TYRELL.

scene 62. In the United Kingdom, most of the Victorian railway system has been irreversibly modernised. We were lucky that one platform of St Pancras Station needed very little to disguise British Rail's embellishments of the nineteenth-century structure. Cardboard pillars, painted as brick, hid the loudspeakers and video monitors which announce the platform's timetable. Poster advertisements were also covered over. On the other platforms, offscreen, the diesel-driven trains arrived and departed. During the brief lulls in between, we filmed.

RICHMOND. Dominic West makes his film début as Richmond. We wanted an upright, handsome, young man whose youth, beauty and assurance Richard could understandably envy. The casting director, Irene Lamb, had been impressed with Dominic when he played Berowne in *Love's Labours Lost* just before he left the Guildhall School of Speech and Drama. His second film is *Surviving Picasso*.

Irene Lamb has often worked with RL. From their work on stage, television and film, she knows well the actors she recommends and when she delivers photos and CVs, she is a staunch advocate. RL liked to judge even very well-known actors for himself, by viewing snippets of their recent screen performances on video-tapes compiled by their agents. Over that hurdle, actors were invited to meet RL, whose enthusiasm invariably encouraged them to accept an offer, if it was made.

PRINCE OF WALES is played by Marco Williamson. Marco is a survivor from the RNT production, when he shared the part of the Prince of Wales's young brother on the US tour.

156

62 EXT. RAILWAY TERMINUS – DAY

A dull-red carpet has been unrolled along the platform, which is empty, except for the small welcoming party in morning-dress, with black arm-bands.

The Royal Train, bringing the heir to the throne, arrives with a screech of powerful brakes, bursting smoke and steam.

PRINCE JAMES is guarded by TYRELL.

HASTINGS waits beside the ARCHBISHOP.

LORD STANLEY has brought along his nephew, HENRY RICHMOND.

The LORD MAYOR OF LONDON, over-dressed in his feathered hat and mayoral chain, is attended by CATESBY.

RICHARD is in top-hat, gloves and morning-dress grey, with black arm-band.

Down from the train, BUCKINGHAM leads his charge, the PRINCE OF WALES, now dressed in the uniform of a junior Admiral of the Fleet.

> RICHARD
> (bowing, all smiles)
> **Welcome, dear nephew.**

The solemn PRINCE OF WALES holds out his hand.

> RICHARD
> (continuing; juggling his top-hat and glove as he shakes hands)
> **Welcome to your capital.**

> PRINCE OF WALES
> **I want more uncles here to welcome me.**

PRINCE JAMES. In the play, on the death of her brother, Queen Elizabeth escaped from Richard's growing power by taking sanctuary with her younger son, in the care of the Church. In this scene, Buckingham persuades the Cardinal to remove the little Prince from sanctuary with the following sophistry:

> Oft have I heard of sanctuary men
> But sanctuary children ne'er till now!

It was a pity to lose this evidence of the Church's complicity in the political manoeuvring of Richard's Protectorship but taking sanctuary is little understood these days.

'For the instalment of this noble Duke,
In the seat royal of our famous land?' This is typical Buckingham language, not quite saying directly what he means, lest one day his words be used in evidence against him.

RICHARD

Those uncles whom you want were dangerous.
Your Highness attended to their sugared words
And looked not on the poison of their hearts.
God keep you from them and from such false
    friends.

PRINCE OF WALES

God keep me from false friends – but they
    were none.

RICHARD

The Prime Minister, Lord Hastings, comes to
    greet you.

PRINCE OF WALES, with HASTINGS, proceeds down
the line, shaking hands.

RICHARD distracts his nephew PRINCE JAMES, as
BUCKINGHAM moves over to CATESBY.

BUCKINGHAM
(privately)
Catesby, is it not an easy matter
To make Lord Hastings of our mind,
For the instalment of this noble Duke,
In the seat royal of our famous land?

CATESBY

He, for the late King's sake, so loves the Prince,
That he will not do anything against him.

BUCKINGHAM

What think you, then, of Lord Stanley? And the
    Archbishop?

RL is checking an angle through the camera's eye-piece. Robert Binnall prepares to measure exactly the distance between me and the lens. He will keep the focus of the picture sharp, wherever the actors may move, by constant adjustments to the camera.

'I think that you should bear me on your shoulders.' Stage directions are rare in Shakespeare but it is likely that with this line he implied that the Prince, who in the play has been handling Richard's dress-sword, should go a leap too far by jumping up on his uncle's deformed back.

In the Olivier film, it was enough for the boy to point at the enlarged shoulder and for Richard to turn murderously round, accompanied by a strident chord on the soundtrack.

CATESBY
They will do all in all as Hastings does.

BUCKINGHAM
Call them tomorrow, early,
To determine of the coronation.
And, as it were far off, sound out Lord
  Hastings.
And give us notice of his inclination.

RICHARD
Commend me to Hastings.
Tell him, Catesby, that Rivers is let blood.

CATESBY, unfazed, nods.

PRINCE JAMES tugs at RICHARD.

RICHARD
(continuing; chuckling and kneeling to the little
boy's level)
What would you have my little Lord?

PRINCE JAMES
Because that I am little like an ape,
I think that you should bear me on your
  shoulders.

PRINCE JAMES leaps up onto RICHARD's hump and is
thrown to the ground. BUCKINGHAM helps PRINCE
JAMES up and dusts him down. LORD STANLEY goes to
help RICHARD, who is pale with shock. A dreadful
embarrassment.

PRINCE OF WALES
I thank you all. Uncle Richard . . .

'Your Highness shall repose you at The Tower.' Richard says this as if The Tower were a swish hotel. In the play, there is here a lengthy exchange about The Tower of London, during which the Prince of Wales irritatingly shows off his knowledge of history.

'Why, what should you fear?'

Holding the door for the little Prince is Steve Morphew who plays Richard's principal bodyguard. He was also my stand-in, taking my place during the lengthy business of lighting a shot, whilst I was able to relax and prepare for the acting ahead.

RICHARD seems to have recovered and joins the PRINCE
OF WALES, followed by PRINCE JAMES with
BUCKINGHAM.

> PRINCE OF WALES
> (continuing)
> **. . . where shall we stay until our coronation?**

> RICHARD
> **If I may counsel you, some day or two,**
> **For your best health and recreation,**
> **Your Highness shall repose you at The Tower.**

> PRINCE JAMES
> **I shall not sleep in quiet at The Tower.**

> RICHARD
> (turning back to PRINCE JAMES)
> **Why, what should you fear?**

> PRINCE JAMES
> **My Uncle Clarence's angry ghost.**
> **My grandma told me he was murdered there.**

> PRINCE OF WALES
> **I fear no uncles dead.**

> RICHARD
> **Nor none who live, I hope.**

The PRINCE OF WALES and PRINCE JAMES are
escorted round the corner of the station building by
TYRELL and GUARDS.

BUCKINGHAM. Jim Broadbent, having starred in RL's *Wide Eyed and Legless* (1993) was his first choice for Buckingham. Other directors, like Richard Eyre, Stephen Frears and Mike Leigh have also cast him again and again on stage and screen. After his success in *Bullets Over Broadway* (1994) will it be long before he works again with Woody Allen? Like many very good actors, he is a uniquely marvellous comedian. As for Buckingham, a part so many have failed in, I had originally expected to cast someone familiar with blank verse. This is Jim's first Shakespeare. That did not worry me, the minute I saw him with his Himmler glasses and his Goering smile.

Richard's car is a 1936 Bentley which spends most weekends carrying newly-weds to and from church.

RICHARD
(continuing; waving his top-hat)
So wise, so young, they say, do never live long.

BUCKINGHAM
(waving too; he puts a hand on RICHARD's arm)
Well let them rest.
My Lord Protector, what shall we do if we perceive
Hastings will not yield to all our plans?

RICHARD
Chop off his head!

BUCKINGHAM can't tell if RICHARD is joking or not.

RICHARD
(continuing)
Something we shall determine.

They walk along the empty platform.

RICHARD
(continuing)
And, look, when I am King, claim you of me
The Earldom of Hereford – and all the movables
Whereof the King, my brother, was possessed.

It's as if BUCKINGHAM has just been promised delivery of the Taj Mahal.

BUCKINGHAM
I'll claim that promise from your royal hand.

scene 63. In his dream, Stanley transfigures Richard into his heraldic boar – the device that will decorate the blackshirt uniforms of his supporters. A foam-latex mask was glued to my face. This had been fashioned on my plaster life-cast in the workshops of Daniel Parker, where there are shelves of unnerving body-parts from Maggie Smith, Robert de Niro and various animals. Tusks lodged on my upper teeth. The porcine contact lenses blinded me once we got them to stay in.

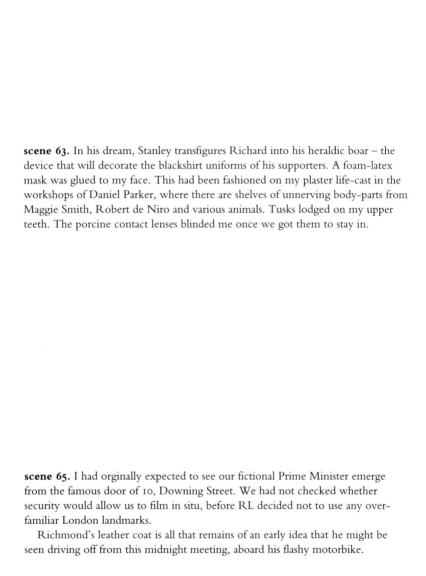

scene 65. I had orginally expected to see our fictional Prime Minister emerge from the famous door of 10, Downing Street. We had not checked whether security would allow us to film in situ, before RL decided not to use any over-familiar London landmarks.

Richmond's leather coat is all that remains of an early idea that he might be seen driving off from this midnight meeting, aboard his flashy motorbike.

RICHARD
(slightly mocking BUCKINGHAM's formality)
**And look to have it yielded with all kindness.
Come, let's to supper.**

LORD STANLEY and RICHMOND watch RICHARD's humped back, as he limps away with BUCKINGHAM.

63   **INT. LORD STANLEY'S NIGHTMARE – DAY**

LORD STANLEY's POV of RICHARD on the ground (as previous scene).

In his dream, LORD STANLEY approaches RICHARD from behind. As he gets closer to the familiar humpback, RICHARD turns to reveal he has the face of a wild boar, slavering and blood-flecked. The savage mouth opens to snarl; the yellow tusks snap at LORD STANLEY, who screams. His cries are drowned by the triumphant squeals and snorts of RICHARD, the boar.

64   **INT. LORD STANLEY'S BEDROOM – NIGHT**

CLOSE on LORD STANLEY's sweating face as he wakes suddenly from his nightmare.

65   **INT. THE PRIME MINISTER'S RESIDENCE –
NIGHT**

At the bottom of the grand staircase, HASTINGS is preparing to go out of the front door, with RICHMOND.

HASTINGS
(yawning)
And then?

LADY HASTINGS. I removed references to Hastings's mistress, Jane Shore, whom he shared with King Edward. (Olivier's film made much of this, with Pamela Browne mysteriously, wordlessly working her way round the throne-room.) It seemed fair to invent a spouse, whose dressing-gown would be a reminder that the Prime Minister is off to a meeting in the middle of the night.

Syon House is very grand for a Prime Minister's official residence, having been presented to the first Duke of Northumberland in 1553. Snooping along the Robert Adam corridors, I found oil portraits of most of the royal cast members of *Richard III*.

scene 67. The Daimler is crossing Southwark Bridge by the church of St Mary Overy (short for 'over-the-river') where Shakespeare's actor brother Edmund was buried in 1607.

RICHMOND
My uncle dreamt tonight 'The Boar' had shown
His tusks. Therefore he sends to know if you
Will shun the danger that his soul does fear.

LADY HASTINGS, in her dressing-gown, is helping her
husband on with his coat.

HASTINGS
(flushed)
Return to Lord Stanley.
Tell him his fears are shallow, wanting
**   substance.**
As for his dreams, I wonder he's so foolish.

HASTINGS blows a kiss to his wife and leaves through the
front door with RICHMOND. CATESBY is waiting in the
back of the Daimler parked outside. The POLICE
CONSTABLE opens the kerbside rear door for HASTINGS
to get in.

HASTINGS
(continuing)
Good morning, Catesby.
(looking out at RICHMOND)
Tell your uncle, I shall see him at the meeting,
Where he shall see 'The Boar' will use us kindly.

67   **INT. DAIMLER – NIGHT**

On its way through the damp London streets.

HASTINGS
Catesby, what news in this our tottering state?

HASTINGS. In the play, William, Lord Hastings, is a senior politician. For the RNT, we had supposed him to be the Prime Minister and David Bradley, playing him in a droopy false moustache, had a resemblance to Neville Chamberlain. In the screenplay, I've risked the purists' disapproval by even calling him 'Prime Minister' every so often. Although as a peer, he would be running the government from the House of Lords, I wondered whether he might have risen to the heights of the power ladder, through the trade union movement.

Jim Carter's strong northern accent clinched it. I have long admired him on stage and screen. Recently he had played another leading politician in *The Madness of King George*, along with Roger Hammond (Archbishop) and, of course, Nigel Hawthorne (Clarence).

'I'll have this crown of mine cut from my shoulders . . .' By now the audience will be alert to the irony of this sort of confidence and suspect that Hastings is, indeed, in for the chop.

scene 69. The tall gates that open for Hastings' car lead into the courtyard of the old headquarters of the Greater London Council.

scene 70. This is the first time that it is obvious that Richard now has his own bodyguards, identified by their black uniforms. This idea was Bob Crowley's for the RNT. Richard's favourite colours are black, white, red and gold.

                    CATESBY
It is a reeling world indeed, sir,
And, I believe, it will never stand upright
Till Richard wear the garland of the state.

                    HASTINGS
How! 'Wear the garland?' Do you mean
   the crown?

                    CATESBY
Yes, my Lord.

                    HASTINGS
I'll have this crown of mine cut from my
   shoulders,
Before I'll see the crown so foul misplaced.

68   **DELETED**

69   **EXT. FORECOURT – LORD PROTECTOR'S
     HEADQUARTERS – NIGHT**

As the car swerves into the forecourt, Big Ben chimes the three-quarter hour.

70   **INT. LOBBY – LORD PROTECTOR'S
     HEADQUARTERS – NIGHT**

HASTINGS self-importantly arrives with CATESBY. Black-uniformed GUARDS protect the lobby. LORD STANLEY is nervously waiting for them at the bottom of the stairs.

                    LORD STANLEY
Hastings . . .

'before a fortnight makes me older . . .' These last lines of the scene, which I had cut, were properly reinstated at the request of Jim Carter and Tim McInnerny. Otherwise I was grateful that apart from the odd line, there were no complaints at all about the substantial cuts, even though they affected all the main characters.

scene 71. This is the Council Chamber within the University of London. An elevator is disguised by a false wall. All the bas reliefs are made of flimsy plaster. From home, I contributed one of the bronze statuettes.

They all start up the staircase.

> HASTINGS
> **Where is your boar-spear, Lord Stanley?**
> (privately to CATESBY)
> **Catesby, before a fortnight makes me older**
> **I'll send some packing that yet think not on it.**

> CATESBY
> **It is a vile thing to die,**
> **When men are unprepared and look not for it.**

71 **INT. LORD PROTECTOR'S OFFICE – NIGHT**

The long room is lit by low, shaded lamps hanging above the circular conference table, which could accommodate 50 but where places are now laid for only 6.

A black-uniformed OFFICER guards the door. The ARCHBISHOP is already there, as the OFFICER smartly opens the door to let in HASTINGS, LORD STANLEY and CATESBY, who tidies papers for the meeting.

> HASTINGS
> (ever jovially)
> **Archbishop, you are early stirring.**

> ARCHBISHOP
> **I am glad to see your honour.**

BUCKINGHAM breezes in from the corridor, in time to see HASTINGS and the ARCHBISHOP shaking hands. He takes his place.

Peter Biziou is checking the effect of his lighting for a close-up of the Archbishop who sits to the left of Jim Carter and his Homburg.

BUCKINGHAM
(good-naturedly)
What! Talking to a priest, Lord Hastings?
Your friend, Earl Rivers, he needed the priest!

HASTINGS laughs confidently.

The ARCHBISHOP misses the joke.

LORD STANLEY is apprehensive.

HASTINGS checks his fob-watch.

HASTINGS
What is it o'clock?

CATESBY
Upon the stroke of two.

HASTINGS
(eager to get on)
Now, gentlemen, the cause why we are met,
Is to determine of the Coronation.

Silence.

HASTINGS
(continuing)
Speak. When is the royal day?

LORD STANLEY
Are all things ready for the royal time?

CATESBY
They are.

BUCKINGHAM
Who knows the Lord Protector's mind in this?

'I have been long a sleeper.' The trick of disadvantaging others by calling a meeting in the early hours was also used by Hitler. Richard has been preparing to be fully alert by having a nap. Until he gets the nod from Buckingham and Catesby, he doesn't know what is required to deal with Hastings. Then, without Buckingham's approval, Richard dangerously improvises.

'Than my Lord Hastings, no man might be bolder.' When the film was being edited, I had one last chance for improvement. In the sound dubbing-studio, I was able to improve my diction and even slightly alter a stress here and there, all synchronised with my mouth movements on the screen. Also, occasional lines could be restored from the play, as here (over a close-up of a smiling Hastings): 'He knows me well and loves me well'.

ARCHBISHOP
(to BUCKINGHAM)
**Your Lordship, we think, should soonest know
his mind.**

BUCKINGHAM
**We know each other's face. For our hearts,
He knows no more of mine than I of yours –
Or I of his, my Lord, than you of mine.
Lord Hastings you and he are near in love.**

HASTINGS
**I have not sounded him
But you, my noble Lords, may name the time
And, on the Duke's behalf, I'll give my voice.**

The OFFICER slams to attention as RICHARD solemnly
enters, followed by TYRELL in a black uniform, the first
recruit in RICHARD's private army of bodyguards.

RICHARD
Good day to all. I have been long a sleeper.

He sits in the Lord Protector's chair. Silence.

BUCKINGHAM
**Had you not come upon your cue, my Lord,
William, Lord Hastings, had pronounced
your part.**

RICHARD
**Than my Lord Hastings, no man might
be bolder.**

Another uncomfortable silence.

'See *how* I am bewitched.' This seems to be the only moment when Shakespeare expects Richard to show any deformity. Elsewhere he discreetly keeps his useless arm and distorted left hand tucked out of sight within specially designed pockets. Kaiser Wilhelm II did the same thing with his left arm. It was not easy to tell from his public appearances that Stalin too had a similar handicap. However, Senator Bob Dole, whose damaged right hand is a war trophy, makes no attempt to hide it.

Richard's flourishing of his claw-like fingers is a staggering piece of bravado. Everyone around the table knows that a congenital deformity must pre-date the influence of Queen Elizabeth or any other 'monstrous witch'. Buckingham and Catesby keep their counsel, although they must be worried that Richard is out of control. Stanley and the Archbishop are prepared to swear black is white if only they can get out of the room alive. As for Hastings, it is the middle of the night and he has had one too many slugs from his whisky flask. His careless 'If' is excuse enough to send him to the gallows.

Tyranny thrives on fear. The major domo conducting visitors into Stalin's office kept spare trousers for those who soiled their own as they waited for admission.

RICHARD
(continuing at last)
I pray you all, tell me what they deserve
Who do conspire my death; and have prevailed
Upon my body, with their damned witchcraft?

HASTINGS
(horrified)
I say, my Lord, they have deserved death.

RICHARD
(rising and rolling up his left sleeve)
See *how* I am bewitched. Behold, my arm
Is like a blasted sapling, withered up –
By Queen Elizabeth, that monstrous witch!

HASTINGS
If she has done this deed, my noble Lord –

RICHARD
(waggling his deformed arm at HASTINGS)
'If'? You protector of this damned Elizabeth –
Talk you to me of 'Ifs'? You are a traitor!
Off with his head. Now, by Saint Paul, I swear
I will not dine, until I see the same.
The rest who love me, rise and follow me.

RICHARD, in apparent rage, limps out.

BUCKINGHAM unhesitatingly follows.

The ARCHBISHOP is ready to vomit and goes next.

LORD STANLEY looks toward CATESBY, who is non-committal. He leaves.

CATESBY, too, goes quickly to catch up with RICHARD, his new boss. HASTINGS is left alone with TYRELL.

scene 72. The deadly drop is too quick for it to be noted that a nerveless double is hanging in place of Jim Carter. He was filmed in a corner of the Spitfire Studios in Middlesex. A wooden cage four storeys high enclosed the pulley, the trap-door and the drop-into-space. The noose's rope was longer than the wire attached to a safety-harness, so that the neck could come to no harm. It did not look safe when he first jumped; which it should not have done, if it were to be convincing in the film. Then the stuntman did it again, with all the lights on and the camera turning. When he asked if the fall had been alright and it was clear he was still alive, all the bystanders applauded. We had seen an execution – and then there was another. RL wanted the body to turn in the light, whilst the stuntman kept his face always away from the camera. I hoped they would not do it again: I should feel obliged to watch again. One execution is very much like another. But RL and Peter Biziou were happy and the stuntman came down and we shook his hand.

'When scarce the blood was well washed from his hands . . .' I had unfeelingly omitted most of this beautiful elegy. After seeing Kristin Scott Thomas be so convincing in scene 23, RL asked me to find some more Shakespeare for her. In the play, this speech (some of which is moved to scene 93) comes just before Anne becomes Queen. Seeing the women gathered away from the men may be a consolation for anyone expecting to hear their long, later scenes of rhetoricised grief, which I judged alien to our film.

TYRELL

**The Duke would be at dinner. He longs to see
your head.**

HASTINGS' eyes show that he still cannot believe his
predicament – as there is a photographer's flash and he drops,
hanged, out of frame.

72   **INT. EXECUTION CHAMBER IN THE TOWER –
      NIGHT**

HASTINGS' corpse jerks, as it drops to the full length of the
hangman's rope.

73   **EXT. GARDENS – THE PALACE – DAY**

The three generations have escaped to the quiet privacy of
the lawn sheltered by the low branches of a spreading
chestnut tree.

The DUCHESS OF YORK is protected by her parasol.
QUEEN ELIZABETH and PRINCESS ELIZABETH are
listening sympathetically to their visitor, who has dropped by
for afternoon tea. LADY ANNE wears a hat and is smoking
nervously. All are still in deep mourning.

LADY ANNE

**When scarce the blood was well washed from
  his hands
Which issued from my other angel-husband;
O when, I say, I looked on Richard's face,
This was my wish : 'Be you', I said, 'accursed!
And when you wed, let sorrow haunt your bed.'
Within so small a time, my woman's heart
Grossly grew captive to his honey words,
And proved the subject of my own soul's curse.**

Here was one of the few opportunities to legitimately open out the scope of the action by filming in an open space. This shot of Bushy Park in Teddington is the traditional view of the beautiful land that Richard wants to call his own. In the first draft of the screenplay, I had had Richard galloping carefree over the South Downs: a horse, a horse.

scene 74. Behind his chair, there is a full-length oil-painting of Richard looking every inch a leader, with two perfectly formed hands, his leather greatcoat around his shoulders (see page 230). For the RNT, Bob Crowley designed a massive backcloth similarly celebrating Richard's heroism. From a quick polaroid, I was painted naked, the left arm wholly restored and held aloft, in the manner of the Third Reich's monumental symbols of manhood. Richard Eyre believed that the penis (although a copy of my own) was ill-proportioned and had it slightly painted over. For the USA, the portrait was again exhibited but modestly clad in a full suit of armour.

LADY ANNE has three new allies, but she feels no better for her confession.

74 **INT. THE LORD PROTECTOR'S OFFICE – DAY**

A GUARD is at the door. CATESBY is standing by, in the sitting area.

RICHARD is obscured by a winged armchair behind an ornate desk. On the wall above is RICHARD's newly installed insignia.

BUCKINGHAM fills an easy chair.

Perched in the middle of a long sofa, the LORD MAYOR examines the black-and-white police photos of HASTINGS' official execution – his neck half-severed by the hangman's noose.

RICHARD swivels round, revealing his new black-shirted uniform.

> RICHARD
> (wiping his eyes)
> **So dear I loved the man that I must weep.**

> BUCKINGHAM
> (an upright liar)
> **Would you believe that the subtle traitor**
> **Had plotted, in the Parliament, to murder me?**

RICHARD clears his throat.

> BUCKINGHAM
> (continuing)
> **. . . and the Lord Protector?**

**'The civil peace
enforced us to this execution.'** Richard intends to avoid a coup d'état by being
voted into power with the approval of the powerful business interests of the City
of London, whose representative is the Lord Mayor.

RL is deciding where the camera will be positioned. At his feet, a member of Peter
Biziou's crew is ready to give the actors our chalk-marked positions on the floor.
Then we can leave the set. Our stand-ins will take our places whilst the electricians
set up their lights.

'Infer the bastardy of Edward's children!' If the two princes were to be
accepted as bastards, Richard could legitimately succeed to the throne. Whether or
not he is slandering King Edward, this reveals Richard's bitterness that he feels
unattractive to women.

**'As if the golden fee for which I plead
Were for myself.'** Buckingham's jokey reminder to Richard that the deal is the
Earldom of Hereford etc.

LORD MAYOR
Had he done so?

RICHARD
The civil peace
Enforced us to this execution.

LORD MAYOR
Now, he deserved his death. And do not doubt
But I'll acquaint my duteous, city colleagues,
With all your just proceedings in this cause.

The LORD MAYOR leaves, CATESBY escorting him to
the door.

RICHARD
Buckingham, go after to the Council House.
Infer the bastardy of Edward's children!
Moreover, urge his hateful lechery,
Which stretched unto their servants,
        daughters, wives.

BUCKINGHAM
(laughing)
Doubt not, my Lord. I'll play the orator
As if the golden fee for which I plead
Were for myself.

BUCKINGHAM leaves. RICHARD calls CATESBY back.

RICHARD
(continuing)
Catesby! Give order that no manner of person
Have any time recourse unto the princes.

CATESBY leaves.

RICHARD re-examines the police photos. Onstage, I had daintily poked a finger into the bloody bucket containing Hastings's severed head. I prefer the film's less messy examination of the execution photos.

scene 75. There was very little chance of removing anything from the edited film which contained text, as it had already been cut to the bone. However, this invented scene (I had contributed 'God!') seemed redundant within the finished assembly and was deleted.

Half-underground.

Alone, RICHARD places a vinyl record on a record player. Cheerful popular music echoes round the office, as RICHARD re-examines the police photos.

75   INT. LOBBY OF THE COUNCIL HOUSE – DAY

The architecture is Victorian Gothic stability, the corridors like naves and the ceilings stretching up to the gods of Commerce and Rectitude. There is no-one about.

There is an increasing murmur of a disorderly meeting from behind a door across the lobby.

From inside, BUCKINGHAM's voice is raised in frustration.

> BUCKINGHAM (V.O.)
> **God!**

BUCKINGHAM bursts through the door, beyond which a full meeting of the City of London has been in session, and makes for the lift. At the doorway, the LORD MAYOR nervously wonders what is now expected of him.

76   EXT. ARENA – EVENING

Half-underground, the Lord Protector's limousine, with RATCLIFFE at the wheel, draws up at the rear entrance to the great Arena, avoiding the CROWDS, whose murmur can be heard, somewhere above.

TYRELL gets out of the car behind and moves forward to help clear a path through the crowd of Press.

Protected by military black-shirted POLICE, BUCKINGHAM is waiting to usher RICHARD into the building.

RICHARD is anxious about what happened at the meeting.

scenes 76–86 were shot over two days, beneath the Earls Court Exhibition Centre in south-west London (Howard Crane, 1936). Buckingham and Catesby have now adopted the uniform of Richard's guards. This followed from Shakespeare's clue that Richard liked dressing-up and was interested in clothes – 'a score or two of tailors' (scene 26) and from the oddest stage direction in Shakespeare: 'Enter Richard and Buckingham in rotten armour, marvellous ill-favoured'(3.5). This sounds like an opinion rather than a description; but it indicates that they are in startling new clothes. From this, Richard Eyre and Bob Crowley supposed they might be in uniform.

scene 77. Richard is impatient for news. Buckingham has failed so far with the City fathers but he has a plan for his client. He does not want Richard waggling his hand at the Lord Mayor, as he had done in scene 71.

The sounds of a great crowd gathering overhead was RL's invention and developed cinematically the impression of a political rally which closed Part One of the RNT production.

RICHARD
What say the citizens?

77 INT. CORRIDOR – BENEATH ARENA – NIGHT

RICHARD and BUCKINGHAM, followed by
RATCLIFFE and TYRELL, stride along the underground
corridors, lined with cladded pipes. Above them, a great
crowd is assembling in the Arena.

BUCKINGHAM tells a long-winded story.

RICHARD
Touched you the bastardy of Edward's children?

BUCKINGHAM
I did.

As BUCKINGHAM continues, RICHARD gets more
tense.

BUCKINGHAM
(continuing)
The insatiate greediness of his desires.
His tyranny for trifles. His own bastardy.
Your discipline in war, wisdom in peace,
Your bounty, virtue, fair humility.
And, when my oratory drew to an end,
I bade those who did love their country's good,
Cry 'God Save King Richard, England's royal
    King!'

RICHARD
And did they so?

BUCKINGHAM
No. So God help me, they spoke not a word.

78   **INT. RECEPTION ROOM – BENEATH ARENA –
     NIGHT**

The décor is pure art deco. This is the star's reception room.
At the other end of the deep carpet is the door to the private
dressing-room.

RATCLIFFE opens the door into the reception room,
where CATESBY is waiting for RICHARD and
BUCKINGHAM.

RICHARD is fuming as he enters.

RICHARD
**What tongueless blocks are they! Would they
not speak?**

A MAKE-UP ARTIST quickly puts down her sherry glass
and the HAIRDRESSER looks up from a lurid romance
novel.

RATCLIFFE closes the door, remaining on guard with
TYRELL in the corridor outside.

CATESBY
**The Lord Mayor and his colleagues have
arrived.**

This stops RICHARD in his tracks.

BUCKINGHAM
Pretend some fear!

Before RICHARD can respond to this astonishing request,
BUCKINGHAM has bundled him through into the

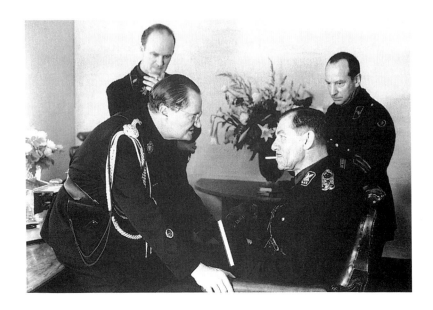

'Play the maid's part – still answer "No" and take it!' With this misogynistic joke Buckingham persuades Richard, for the first time in his life, to do what he is told. 'High-reaching Buckingham' is flying and Richard is looking forward to his own contribution. They are a great team.

dressing-room. CATESBY indicates that the MAKE-UP ARTIST and HAIRDRESSER should stay put in the reception room and then follows RICHARD and BUCKINGHAM and closes the door.

79   INT. DRESSING-ROOM – BENEATH ARENA – NIGHT

Another stylish room, with every comfort for the visiting celebrity. Sofas and side-tables with nibbles, drinks, newspapers and massive floral displays. RICHARD paces dangerously.

> BUCKINGHAM
> **And, look you, get a prayerbook in your hand.**
> **Be not easily won by our requests.**
> **Play the maid's part – still answer 'No' and take**
>   **it!**

RICHARD likes the idea. CATESBY takes in the plan.

> BUCKINGHAM
> **Ratcliffe!**

> RICHARD
> **No doubt we will bring it to a happy issue.**

> BUCKINGHAM
> **You shall see what I can do.**

CATESBY opens the door and lets in the MAKE-UP ARTIST and HAIRDRESSER. BUCKINGHAM leaves with CATESBY, to meet the LORD MAYOR who RATCLIFFE has admitted to the reception room. The MAKE-UP ARTIST begins to give RICHARD the beautification treatment.

scene 80. The underground room at Earls Court had no atmosphere until the art department added its wall panels (9 feet x 4 feet) each with a legend from the play e.g.: 'This Noble Isle', 'Glorious Summer', over an appropriate poster to encourage the nation's shipbuilding and harvesting (see page 190).

This transformation reminded me of recently visiting a Hollywood office which had once been a film studio. In the inner courtyard there were still wooden staircases leading up to the old dressing-rooms. One of these had been used by Humphrey Bogart. It was where *Casablanca* had been filmed. I rushed down the steps and peered through the window of the doors into the cellar that some fifty years before had been Rick's Café. All I could see was a characterless space filled with piles of discarded paperwork, detritus of the electronic revolution. The door was locked and there was no point in asking for the key.

INT. RECEPTION ROOM – BENEATH ARENA – NIGHT

The LORD MAYOR has persuaded a dozen distinguished-looking BANKERS and CIVIC LEADERS from the Council House to meet RICHARD. They are men of the world, somewhat reluctantly here. They will take some convincing. We recognise LORD STANLEY, RICHMOND and the ARCHBISHOP. RATCLIFFE, checking everyone is present, retires to the corridor. The charade begins.

> CATESBY
> (politely but firmly)
> **He does entreat you, my Lord Buckingham,**
> **To visit him tomorrow, or next day.**
> **He is within, with two right reverend priests.**

> BUCKINGHAM
> **Tell him, myself, the Mayor, and these**
> **gentlemen**
> **Are come to have some conference with him.**

> CATESBY
> (doubtfully)
> **I'll tell him what you say, my Lord.**

CATESBY knocks and goes into the dressing-room, smartly, so no-one can see inside.

> BUCKINGHAM
> **Ah ha, Lord Mayor. Richard is not King**
> **Edward.**
> **He is not lulling on a lewd love-bed,**
> **But meditating with two deep divines . . .**

scene 81. Ratcliffe is left inside the dressing-room with the make-up and hair artists, so that he could remain innocent of Richard's deceitfulness.

81 INT. DRESSING-ROOM – BENEATH ARENA – NIGHT

A dab of powder completes the make-up. Brylcreem is applied.

> BUCKINGHAM
> (continuing V.O.)
> **. . . and praying, to enrich his watchful soul.**
> **Happy were England, would this virtuous man,**
> **Take on his Grace the sovereignty thereof.**

82 INT. RECEPTION ROOM – BENEATH ARENA – NIGHT

> LORD MAYOR
> **God defend Richard should say 'No' to us.**

> BUCKINGHAM
> **I fear he will.**

CATESBY returns.

> BUCKINGHAM
> (continuing)
> **Catesby?**

> CATESBY
> **He wonders to what end you have assembled**
> **Such troops of citizens to speak with him.**
> **My Lord, he fears you mean no good to him.**

> BUCKINGHAM
> **By Heaven, we come to him in perfect love.**

A couple of them seem to agree with that.

scene 84. In my first draft, I had adopted Shakespeare's outdoor setting.

EXT. INNER COURTYARD OF THE PALACE – NIGHT

A wintry scene – a sprinkling of snow on the cobblestones. Gaslamps throw pools of soft, yellow light below an impressive balcony of granite.

A group of up to a hundred ALDERMEN, in winter coats, hats, gloves and scarves, are tentatively gathering, quietly and expectantly chatting to each other. In the shadows, beneath the arches surrounding the courtyard, Richard's troops, in black, silently assemble.

The balcony is dazzlingly lit by floodlights. Two priests and a Commander-in-Chief at prayer.

Olivier's film did something similar, providing himself with the startling slide down the rope, which sets all the bells of London clanging with acclamation. Within our modernised setting, RL contained the scene within less theatrical confines. Having the city deputation close-to, I was under pressure to be a really convincing liar. I slipped on Richard's reading glasses, which had my prescription in period frames, to suggest a placid bookworm, despite the black uniform.

'Not as Lord Protector, but from blood to blood –' Richard will never have an heir to whom he could pass on the throne. Kristin Scott Thomas and I agreed that Lady Anne and Richard did not have sex after their first unsuccessful attempt – offscreen!

83 DELETED

84 INT. RECEPTION ROOM – BENEATH ARENA – NIGHT

BUCKINGHAM opens the door to the dressing-room a crack and calls to RICHARD.

> BUCKINGHAM
> **My Lord Protector, pray pardon us**
> **The interruption of your devotions.**

RICHARD enters modestly, prayer-book in hand. The room falls expectantly silent. BUCKINGHAM acts relieved but apprehensive.

> RICHARD
> **My Lord, there needs no such apology.**
> **I do suspect I have done some offence.**

> BUCKINGHAM
> **You have! Will it please you to amend**
>   **your fault?**

> RICHARD
> **Else wherefore breathe I in a Christian land?**

> BUCKINGHAM
> **Know then, it is your fault that you refuse**
> **The supreme seat, the throne majestical.**
> **We heartily solicit you take on**
> **The kingly government of this your land,**
> **Not as Lord Protector, but from blood**
>   **to blood –**
> **Your right of birth, your empery, your own.**

'First, if all obstacles were cut away . . .' Richard allows himself his little private joke, which the audience can share because they have seen Clarence and Rivers both cut away. The line is phrased comically – the long sound of 'were' gives Richard time to think how he can best put it; a half-pause that leads to the ironic euphemism of 'cut away'.

RICHARD
Your love deserves my thanks; but my desert,
Unmeritable, shuns your high request.

Disappointment.

RICHARD
(continuing)
First, if all obstacles were cut away,
Yet, so much is my poverty of spirit,
So mighty and so many my defects,
That I would rather hide me from my
     greatness.
But, God be thanked, there is no need of me.
The royal tree has left us royal fruit –

BUCKINGHAM
(interrupting)
– You say the Prince of Wales is your
     brother's son?

RICHARD nods.

BUCKINGHAM
(continuing)
So say we too – but born before his
     wedding day!

RICHARD looks appalled at this slander.

BUCKINGHAM
(continuing)
Then, good my Lord, take to your royal self
This proffered benefit of dignity.

LORD MAYOR
O, good my Lord Protector . . . !

'Truly, the hearts of men are full of fear.' This line is transposed from a scene in the play (2.3) where three citizens, on their way to a council meeting, discuss the recent death of King Edward and the impending doom of Richard's Lord Protectorship.

Roger Hammond plays the Archbishop. He and I were both born and bred in the north of England. We met in 1958 at Cambridge University, acting together with undergraduate dramatic societies. As professionals, we have both been beneficiaries of the influence that Cambridge graduates had on British Theatre in the Sixties and Seventies, through the actors, directors, managers and drama critics who shared the same academic training and cultural assumptions.

e.g.: my first Shakespeare, *Richard II*, was directed by Richard Cottrell (Cambridge 1957–60) and produced by Toby Robertson (1950–2). My first season for the RSC was directed by Trevor Nunn (1959–61) and John Barton (who, when a postgraduate at Cambridge, had directed Roger, me, David Frost, Derek Jacobi, Terrence Hardiman, Richard Cottrell and John Tydeman, a future head of Drama for BBC Radio). For the RNT, I played Coriolanus for Peter Hall (1954–7) and Richard III for Richard Eyre (1962–65).

CITY GENTLEMAN
We entreat you.
Refuse not, Gloucester, this proffered love!

ARCHBISHOP
(*sotto voce* to LORD STANLEY)
Truly, the hearts of men are full of fear.

RICHARD
I am unfit for state and majesty.

BUCKINGHAM
Then we will plant some other on the throne!

RICHARD
I do beseech you take it not amiss.
I cannot, nor I will not, yield to you!

BUCKINGHAM
(making to leave)
Your brother's son will never reign our king!
Gentlemen, come! I will entreat no more. God's
    wounds!

RICHARD
O, do not swear, my lord of Buckingham!

The CITY GENTLEMEN look as if they will leave with
BUCKINGHAM.

CATESBY
Call him again, My Lord. Accept the crown.

RICHARD
Will you enforce me to a world of cares?
Call him again.

'I am not made of stone.' Just as onstage an actor's attention is balanced between relating to the other actors and being aware of the audience's reaction, when filming you are never exclusively concentrating on the action, unless the camera is so far away that it can be ignored. At this point, finding myself close to the lens, as if it were another player in the scene, it seemed appropriate to treat it as a participant and address this line directly.

'Since you will buckle fortune on my back . . .' is a sly reference to his deformed spine, as Richard plays the sympathy card.

Perhaps for the first time, Buckingham has discovered excitement in his life. His mistake is to think that he will ever again be able to control an ego the size of Richard's.

CATESBY goes toward BUCKINGHAM who turns back.

>   RICHARD
>   (continuing)
> **I am not made of stone.**
> **Since you will buckle fortune on my back,**
> **I must have patience to endure the load.**

The CITY GENTLEMEN are pleased at their powers
of persuasion.

>   RICHARD
>   (continuing)
> **But God doth know, and you may partly see,**
> **How far I am from the desire of this.**

RICHARD walks out, accompanied by BUCKINGHAM.

85   **INT. CORRIDOR – BENEATH ARENA – NIGHT**

CATESBY ushers the GENTLEMEN out through the door,
as RICHARD acknowledges them in turn.

BUCKINGHAM leads them down the corridor to the Arena
above, accompanied by RATCLIFFE and TYRELL.

LORD STANLEY, with RICHMOND and the
ARCHBISHOP, follows behind.

RICHARD pauses for a moment, then turns and walks
down the opposite corridor.

86   **INT. RECEPTION ROOM – BENEATH ARENA –**
      NIGHT

The sound of the amassed CROWD drowns the rumble of
the escalators as BUCKINGHAM, RATCLIFFE, TYRELL

scene 87.

A press release was broadcast on local radio: 'Anyone over 16 who is interested in helping with the crucial scene where Richard accepts the title of King of England should present themselves at 3.00pm on Monday 31 July, at Hall no. 2, The Royal Horticultural Hall, Greycoat Street, London SW1.

'You should wear a dark-coloured jacket or shirt or T-shirt and be prepared to spend 3 hours filming. You need never have acted but because of the film's historical period you should be light-skinned.

'There is no payment.'

Two hundred people responded and were grouped in a corner of the art deco Hall. They included my sister Jean, who is a keen amateur actor and director (one of her earliest performances at Wigan High School for Girls was as Bottom in *A Midsummer Night's Dream*) and her husband Foster, as well as my friends, neighbours and Liam, the manager of my local bar. Kristin Scott Thomas and I were there too, with others from the crew. We waved our banners, shouted and saluted. Then we were moved in changed formations around the Hall to be filmed again. The varying shots were electronically re-assembled so that we seemed to fill the Hall which, by further trick photography, was expanded to three times its actual length.

Our repeated chant of 'Amen!' (3.7) was changed in the final cut to 'Richard!' Onstage, I had acknowledged my subjects with a full-arm salute but in the film did not want to specifically identify Richard with fascism.

and the CITY GENTLEMEN make their way up to the Arena above.

LORD STANLEY hesitates behind, with RICHMOND and the ARCHBISHOP.

>   ARCHBISHOP
> **If you will outstrip death, go cross the seas**
> **And live, dear Richmond, from the reach**
> **   of Hell.**

>   LORD STANLEY
> **Go, my dear nephew, from this slaughterhouse.**

LORD STANLEY and the ARCHBISHOP shake hands with RICHMOND, and alight the escalators. RICHMOND watches them for a moment, then turns and walks back down the corridor.

CATESBY has observed this parting, as he waits to conduct the ARCHBISHOP and LORD STANLEY up to the Arena. The crowd above is sounding increasingly enthusiastic.

87   INT. ARENA – NIGHT

The Arena is packed with thousands of RICHARD'S SUPPORTERS, male and female, young and old, civilian and blackshirts. On the platform, DRUMMERS AND TRUMPETERS are lined behind the CITY GENTLEMEN, all in place. The last to enter are the ARCHBISHOP and LORD STANLEY, looking somewhat appalled at the vast crowd.

On BUCKINGHAM's entrance onstage, the place erupts. He approaches the podium, bristling with microphones.

BUCKINGHAM
Long live King Richard!

There is a gasp of delight at this unexpected announcement.
The trumpets sound the percussive martial music which
RICHARD played to himself in his office.

The mighty arc-lights swing across the heads of the crowd,
signifying that the Lord Protector has arrived in the
auditorium. As RICHARD slowly marches onstage, from
up-centre, the entire audience rises and cheers and waves. A
CHILD breaks ranks and throws RICHARD a posy of
flowers. Film cameras whirr. Flaming torches are lit.

EVERYONE
Amen! Amen! Amen! Amen! Amen!

As RICHARD reaches the podium, the orgiastic climax
surpasses itself.

RICHARD acknowledges his subjects with a dazzling smile
and as he raises his good arm in greeting, behind him his new
flag unfurls – red, white and black. RICHARD is happy for
the last time in his life.

88 **EXT. GATEWAY TO THE TOWER – DAY**

QUEEN ELIZABETH and her daughter PRINCESS
ELIZABETH, with the DUCHESS OF YORK and LADY
ANNE, all wrapped up in furs against the cold, have arrived
to see the Princes in The Tower. The grown-ups are in
mourning and veiled. Two limousines have brought them to
The Tower's entrance.

BRACKENBURY stands behind the massive iron gate,
respectful and overwhelmed by this royal visitation. QUEEN
ELIZABETH is confident she will gain admission to
The Tower.

scene 88. From within the Bankside power station where this scene was shot, a constant electrical hum almost drowned the dialogue, all of which had to be re-voiced in a sound studio.

'I am their mother.' The real princes were 13 and 9 years old when they disappeared in 1483. Nearly 200 years later, the bones of two children were excavated within The Tower and re-buried in Westminster Abbey.

'I am bound by oath and therefore pardon me.' This sort of plea was not considered admissable at the Nuremberg Trials. It is an unenviable job caring for political prisoners, of whatever age, and treating them like common criminals.

QUEEN ELIZABETH
Brackenbury, how are my sons, the Princes?

BRACKENBURY
Right well, Your Majesty.

QUEEN ELIZABETH steps forward to the entrance but
BRACKENBURY stops her.

BRACKENBURY
(continuing)
**By your patience, I may not permit you to
visit them.**
The King has strictly charged the contrary.

QUEEN ELIZABETH
'The King!' Who's that?

BRACKENBURY
I mean the Lord Protector.

QUEEN ELIZABETH
The Lord protect him from that kingly title.
**I am their mother. Who should keep me
from them?**

DUCHESS OF YORK
I am their father's mother. I will see them.

LADY ANNE
I am their aunt. Then bring us to their sight.

BRACKENBURY
(deeply embarrassed)
I am bound by oath and therefore, pardon me.

'Rude, ragged nurse, use my babies well.'

scene 90. The visual climax of Richard's ascent is the invented scene at the Rally (scene 87). The Coronation, another scene not in the play, is used by RL to show the decline of Lady Anne, through whose eyes we watch the enthronement. At one time, I was expecting a day's filming in Westminster Abbey. This was too complicated to organise and, as it turned out, unnecessary. We used a corner of St John the Baptist's Church in west London, with convincing replicas of the genuine Coronation paraphernalia. The Sword of State and the Sceptre had to be clutched together in Richard's one good hand.

The ladies turn toward their limousines.

> DUCHESS OF YORK
> (to LADY ANNE)
> **Go you to Richard – and good angels guard**
> **you!**

The CHAUFFEUR opens the car door for LADY ANNE,
who looks more haggard than ever.

> QUEEN ELIZABETH
> (sobbing)
> **Stay yet. Look back with me unto The Tower.**
> **Pity, you ancient stones, those tender princes**
> **Whom envy has immured within your walls.**
> **Rough cradle for such little pretty ones.**
> **Rude, ragged nurse, use my babies well.**

89   INT. LADY ANNE'S LIMOUSINE – DAY

Alone in the back, LADY ANNE hitches up her skirt and
finds the appropriate spot in her much-punctured thigh. She
injects herself with a calming drug. Then she closes her eyes
and waits for it to work.

Over, the triumphal, martial orchestrations of celebration.

90   INT. THE CATHEDRAL – DAY

The time-honoured glory of the Coronation reaches its
climax – musically and visually.

Everyone of any importance seems to have squeezed into the
medieval cathedral. Dusty, threadworn, military banners hang
from the hammerbeam roof. The PEERS and their
PEERESSES wear ermined coronets, bejewelled tiaras and
scarlet velvet robes.

Craig Bloor was our Clapper Loader, the junior member of the camera team who loads the film and cares for it and starts each shot by clapping a stick down onto the board that records the scene number, thereby synchronising sound and film. Craig's clapping was always gently unobtrusive, a welcome change from others I have known who place their board up against the actor's face, as if hoping to trap a nose as they clap.

scene 91. This 4½-minute scene was shot without a break, as the camera slid in front of the actors, at Eltham Palace in south-east London.

RL was impressed that the actors didn't fluff their lines or stumble over their moves, until I pointed out that we are used to even longer takes on stage; as long, that is, as the Act between the opening line and the curtain call. Here, it is the actors' own timing which carries the scene, without the later intervention of the film's editor.

Whether an audience realises the unusual length of the take does not matter; but perhaps they will sense the relentless way in which the camera observes Richard's confidence cracking in front of their eyes.

Fortnum's chocolates. Hitler enjoyed watching newsreel of his public appearances in the company of his inner circle. He was also partial to sticky chocolates. I discovered this when playing the Führer in the drama/documentary *Countdown to War* (Granada TV: 1989).

Tradition and ritual confirm the legitimacy of RICHARD III's struggle to the throne, where in the distance he is now crowned by the ARCHBISHOP, with LADY ANNE as his Queen.

91 **INT. PRIVATE VIEWING THEATRE – NIGHT**

A pillared art deco hall has been fitted out with screen and projector, to make a private cinema.

Next to matching armchairs for the KING and QUEEN, BUCKINGHAM proudly sits. There are rows of gilded, plush, upright chairs for BRACKENBURY, CATESBY, RATCLIFFE, LORD STANLEY and TYRELL.

The music continues over the black-and-white propaganda film which is viewed, with appreciative applause at times, by the new KING'S COURTIERS, all uniformed in black.

There is an air of lassitude and fear. No-one dares to cross RICHARD, yet no-one knows what he wants, until he tells them.

The doleful LADY ANNE sits upright and pale, next to RICHARD, who is munching Fortnum's chocolates. He leans across to BUCKINGHAM, with brandy and cigar. The music keeps the conversations private.

> RICHARD
> **Now Buckingham! Thus high, by your advice**
> **And your assistance, is King Richard seated.**
> **But shall we wear these glories for a day?**
> **Or shall they last and we rejoice in them?**

> BUCKINGHAM
> **Still live they and for ever let them last.**

'Why, Buckingham, I say I would be King.' Richard does not say what kind of king. Throughout, he has a need to be active, to re-create the excitement of fighting in his civilian life. He has no credo and his kingship is politically barren. His only concern is to hold onto his new power, not to use it for the benefit of his subjects. Although the film uses the iconography of fascism, Richard is a dictator pure and simple, from neither the right nor the left. The fascistic references are a reminder that an English dictatorship (even by a Royal claimant) is credible within the 1930s setting.

'Buckingham, you never used to be so dull.' This is my translation of 'Cousin, thou wast not wont to be so dull' (4.2).

RICHARD

The Princes live. Think now what I would speak.

BUCKINGHAM

Say on, Your Majesty.

RICHARD

Why, Buckingham, I say I would be King.

BUCKINGHAM

Why so you are.

RICHARD

The princes live.
Buckingham, you never used to be so dull.
Shall I be plain? I wish the bastards dead.
And I would have it suddenly performed.
What say you now?

Silence.

RICHARD
(continuing)

Speak suddenly – be brief.

BUCKINGHAM
(rising)

Your Majesty may do your pleasure.

RICHARD

Tut, tut, you are all ice. Your kindness freezes.
Say, have I your consent that they shall die?

BUCKINGHAM
(bowing)
Give me some little breath, some pause,
Your Majesty,
Before I positively speak in this.

BUCKINGHAM retires to consider his position.

RICHARD
(to CAMERA)
High-reaching 'Buck-ing-ham' grows
circumspect.
Has he so long held out with me untired
And stops he now for breath. Well, be it so.
(aloud)
Lord Stanley!

LORD STANLEY
(moving up behind RICHARD)
Your Majesty?

RICHARD
What's the news?

LORD STANLEY
The Archbishop, as I hear,
Has joined with Richmond, Your Majesty,
in France.

RICHARD
Richmond aims to marry young Elizabeth,
My brother Edward's daughter.
By that knot, he hopes to get my crown.
Richmond is your nephew. Well, look to it.

'Tyrell!' In the play, this is the first appearance of Tyrell, the 'discontented gentleman', who is recruited by King Richard to dispatch the princes in The Tower. Although it is said that gold will 'tempt him to anything', Tyrell employs two others to do these murders. All three are appalled at the 'piteous massacre'. Tyrell tells the tale in a 23-line soliloquy to the audience, which Richard does not hear. He invites Tyrell to

> . . . come to me soon at after-supper,
> When you shall tell the story of their death.

What transpires at this intimate, late-evening rendezvous, Shakespeare does not reveal and Tyrell leaves the play. Richard Eyre extended the part as far as the battle, where Tyrell is one of Richard's inner circle, along with Ratcliffe and Norfolk, another adjutant who is missing from the film.

It seemed credible that the ever-obliging Tyrell could engineer all the murders. As in the play, Richard half-befriends his accomplice. Their relationship contrasts with the professional reserve which separates Richard from his other intimate, Ratcliffe.

In Adrian Dunbar's perfectly judged performance, Tyrell likes taking orders not just because he is a loyalist but because he relishes his cunning as an assassin. Not just a thug, he takes pride in a job well done. He likes being close to Richard – amorality and ambition are a lethal combination. They remain dependent on each other to the end.

LORD STANLEY hears the warning and withdraws.

> RICHARD
> (calling outloud)
>
> **Catesby!**

CATESBY, ever the King's private secretary, leans close to
RICHARD.

> RICHARD
> (continuing)
>
> **Rumour it abroad**
> **That Anne, my wife, is very grievous sick.**
> **Look how you dream! I say again, give out**
> **That Anne, my queen, is sick – and like to die.**

LADY ANNE is in a drugged world of her own. Stunned,
CATESBY leaves the room.

> RICHARD
> (continuing)
>
> **Tyrell!**
> (to CAMERA)
>
> **I must be married to my brother's daughter,**
> **Or else my kingdom stands on brittle glass.**
> **Murder her brothers and then marry her.**

TYRELL arrives and stands by RICHARD's chair.
RICHARD beckons him closer.

> RICHARD
> (continuing *sotto voce*)
>
> **Dare you resolve to kill a friend of mine?**

> TYRELL
>
> **Please you; but I'd rather kill two enemies.**

'It is done, Your Majesty.' Unlike Buckingham, Tyrell does not seem to hesitate at the suggestion of infanticide. He is rewarded with the promise of Richard's 'love' – a rare commodity, only otherwise mentioned when Richard seduces Lady Anne.

RICHARD
Why, there you have it. Two deep enemies.
Tyrell . . .
(into his ear)
. . . I mean those bastards in The Tower.
Say it is done, and I will love you for it.

TYRELL
It is done, Your Majesty.

As BUCKINGHAM returns, RICHARD dismisses
TYRELL, who leaves the room. BUCKINGHAM stands
provocatively between RICHARD and the screen.

BUCKINGHAM
(loud)
Your Majesty, I claim the Earldom of Hereford,
The which you promised I should possess.
The court tries not to appear to listen.

RICHARD
Well, let that rest.

RICHARD rises and moves away to the long windows that
lead onto the balcony.

RICHARD
(continuing)
The Archbishop's fled to Richmond.

BUCKINGHAM follows RICHARD out onto the balcony.

BUCKINGHAM
I hear the news.

'Riche–monde!' Richard contains his fear about Richmond and Buckingham by mocking their names: 'Bucking-*ham*' and, here, 'Riche-monde', a disparaging reference to his forces being marshalled in France. Lady Thatcher privately referred to her principal opponent as 'Kin-*nock*'.

**EXT. BALCONY – PRIVATE VIEWING THEATRE
– NIGHT**

Backed by a massive clock, the large balcony looks out onto
the twinkling lights of the capital city. Traffic sounds below.
The two old allies stand side by side. Behind them, the film
continues to be projected.

> BUCKINGHAM
> (continuing)
> **What says Your Majesty to my just request?**

> RICHARD
> **As I remember, it was prophesied,**
> **That Richmond should be King! A king!**
>   **Perhaps . . .**

> BUCKINGHAM
> (more insistent)
> **Your promise for the Earldom!**

> RICHARD
> (a mocking pronunciation)
> **Riche – monde!**

> BUCKINGHAM
> **Your Majesty –**

> RICHARD
> **Yes! What's o'clock?**

> BUCKINGHAM
> **I am thus bold to put Your Majesty in mind**
> **Of what you promised me.**

'**Upon the stroke of ten.**' The clock on the façade of the Shell-Mex House overlooks the Thames and is reputedly the largest in Europe. Throughout the evening we filmed, its hands were fixed at 10 o'clock. As it does not strike, the chimes were added later. Ironically we could only film (and record sound) between the quarter-hour booms of Big Ben, as it kept proper time a half-mile upstream above the Houses of Parliament.

Here was another opportunity for Richard to appear shorter.

'**And is it thus?**' This brief speech was cut because Jim Broadbent's expressive face said it all. Their partnership was never an equal one – although it takes half-a-dozen murders for Buckingham to realise that Richard has an agenda that does not include both of them. He has compromised and worked harder than ever in his charmed life, to help 'Buckingham/Gloucester Inc.' to succeed. He might even collude in infanticide, if only Richard would hand over the reward he has promised. But there is no honour, even among titled thieves.

RICHARD
Well: but what's o'clock?

BUCKINGHAM
(consulting his fob watch)
Upon the stroke of ten.

RICHARD
Well, let it strike.

BUCKINGHAM
Why let it strike?

RICHARD
Because that, like a Jack, you keep the stroke
Between your begging and my meditation.
I am not in the giving vein today.

BUCKINGHAM
Why then, resolve me whether you will or no.

RICHARD
You trouble me. I am not in the vein!

The clock behind them deafeningly chimes ten.

RICHARD strides back into the room, which he leaves,
followed obediently by BRACKENBURY, RATCLIFFE
and LORD STANLEY.

BUCKINGHAM
And is it thus? Repays he my deep service
With such contempt?

BUCKINGHAM shivers and goes back into the room.

'**O never yet one hour in his bed,**
Have I enjoyed the golden dew of sleep . . .' Another foretaste of Macbeth
who murders sleep, and of his wife, who sleep-walks. It is a telling insight that
Richard has regular nightmares, leading up to the night before the battle when his
final dream is dramatised.

scene 94.

93 INT. PRIVATE VIEWING THEATRE – NIGHT

BUCKINGHAM, thinking he is alone, slumps in the nearest chair.

>   LADY ANNE
> **O never yet one hour in his bed,**
> **Have I enjoyed the golden dew of sleep;**
> **But have been wakened by his timorous**
>   **dreams.**
> **Besides, he hates me:**
> **And will, no doubt, shortly be rid of me.**

>   BUCKINGHAM
> **O, let me think of Hastings and be gone.**

BUCKINGHAM looks at LADY ANNE. They have both been duped by RICHARD. But there is no time to sympathise.

BUCKINGHAM has decided to escape, leaving LADY ANNE alone, catatonic.

94 INT. THE PRINCES' CELL – THE TOWER – DAY

TYRELL holds a tightly woven, red silk scarf over the face of PRINCE JAMES. As the victim gasps for air, the silk is drawn into his mouth and deep into the throat.

95 INT. GRAND STAIRCASE – THE PALACE – DAY

QUEEN ELIZABETH sits alone on the stairs. The shock of her sons' death fills her heart and will not be released until she faces the man who ordered their murder.

96 INT. THE KING'S OFFICE – DAY

RICHARD is seated at his desk. An impressive self-portrait of him in his new black uniform dominates the room.

TYRELL enters.

> RICHARD
> **Kind Tyrell. Am I happy in your news?**

> TYRELL
> **It's done, Your Majesty.**

> RICHARD
> **But did you see them dead?**

> TYRELL
> **I did, Your Majesty.**

> RICHARD
> **And buried, gentle Tyrell?**

TYRELL nods.

> RICHARD
> (continuing)
> **Come to me, Tyrell . . . soon . . . at after-supper,**
> **When you shall tell the story of their death.**
> **Meanwhile, but think how I may do you good:**
> **And be inheritor of your desire.**
> **Till then . . .**

TYRELL leaves, and RICHARD, left alone, turns to look at his image on the wall behind.

'I am in
So far in blood, that sin will pluck on sin': cf. Macbeth's
'I am in blood
Stepped in so far, that should I wade no more,
Returning were as tedious as go o'er.'(3.4)
Richard's confession that he has sinned is put aside by his determination to control
the conscience which will erupt in his nightmare in scene 110.

scene 97. Shakespeare does not make it clear how Anne dies – an overdose
perhaps or does Tyrell pay her a visit? Whichever way, Richard is responsible for
her fatal decline.

Queen Elizabeth calls Richard 'a bottled spider' (scene 41). I saw Robert
Helpmann as Richard III mount the Old Vic stage (1957) in front of a backcloth
painted with a huge spider's web. Tony Sher for the RSC (1984), on crutches and
with long, dangling sleeves, also invited arachnoid comparisons. Here, film of a
model spider was superimposed on a static shot of Kristin Scott Thomas's face.

scene 98. Mezzanine of the Senate House.

RICHARD
(continuing)
The sons of Edward sleep in Abraham's bosom;
And Anne – my wife – shall bid the world
    good night.
Uncertain way of gain. But I am in
So far in blood, that sin will pluck on sin.
Tear-falling pity dwells not in this eye.

97   **INT. LADY ANNE'S BEDROOM – THE PALACE –**
     DAY

The heavy curtains are drawn, but a crack of sunlight from
the middle slices across the room. ANNE lies in her bed. She
seems to be staring at a large black spider that drops slowly
on its thread from above her.

The spider lands on LADY ANNE's pale face and crawls
delicately across one unblinking eye.

98   **INT. CORRIDOR OUTSIDE THE KING'S OFFICE**
     – DAY

The door to the King's office opens and RICHARD, dressed
in his black leather greatcoat, cap, gloves and carrying his
officer's baton, strides out into the corridor with TYRELL.

As they walk across the galleried landing towards the stairs,
RATCLIFFE appears and calls after RICHARD.

RATCLIFFE
Your Majesty!

RICHARD
Ratcliffe.

'You toad!' This epithet echoes Queen Margaret: 'this poisonous bunch-backed toad' (1.3).

In the play, the Duchess of York and Queen Elizabeth bewail with Queen Margaret, as they await Richard's departure for war. Onstage, we called it 'the Greenham Common' scene. It has 135 lines before the women confront the man they all hate. Some of the deleted lines of Queen Margaret have been given to the Duchess. Queen Elizabeth's subsequent exchange with Richard is delayed until scene 101.

RATCLIFFE
**Upon the southern coast, there rides a
  powerful navy.
It's thought that Richmond is its admiral.
Buckingham has fled, to welcome him ashore.**

RICHARD
We must be brief when traitors brave the field!

Before RATCLIFFE has time to leave, the DUCHESS OF
YORK appears at the top of the stairs.

DUCHESS OF YORK
Are you my son?

RICHARD is startled by her voice but recovers.

RICHARD
Yes, I thank God, my father and yourself!

DUCHESS OF YORK
**You toad! Where are the Princes? And
  your wife?**

RICHARD
**Mother, I have a touch of your condition,
That cannot bear the accent of reproof.**

No-one has invited RATCLIFFE and TYRELL to leave.
They observe stony-faced.

DUCHESS OF YORK
O, let me speak.

RICHARD
Be brief, good Mother, for I am in haste.

'You came on earth to make the earth my hell.' cf. Lady Anne's 'You have made the happy earth my hell' (scene 23).

Whatever justice there is in the Duchess of York's disaffection towards her youngest son, it is based on her disappointment and disgust at his physique. Perhaps it was from his mother that Richard learnt how to hate so fiercely.

.

DUCHESS OF YORK
(ignoring TYRELL and RATCLIFFE)
A grievous burden was your birth to me.

RICHARD
(who has heard this before)
And came I not, at last, to comfort you?

DUCHESS OF YORK
You came on earth to make the earth my hell.
Tetchy and wayward was your infancy;
Your schooldays frightful, desperate, wild
  and furious;
Your prime of manhood daring, bold and
  venturous;
Your age confirmed, proud, subtle, sly
  and bloody.
What comfortable hour can you name,
That ever graced me with your company?

RICHARD
(dismissively)
If I be so disgracious in your eye –

DUCHESS OF YORK
– Hear me a word!
For I shall never speak to you again.

RICHARD
(looking directly at her)
So?

'To war take with you my most grievous curse!' Richard is speechless at his mother's insistent prayer that he should die in battle. As she leaves, he is aware that the family row has been witnessed by Ratcliffe and Tyrell.

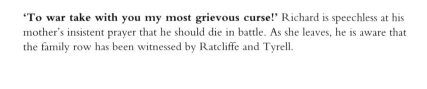

scene 99. Shoreham Aerodrome is a relic from early passenger flight. It was a part of the nation's defence against enemy air attack in the Second World War. These days, it services private planes, flying teachers and their pupils. We shot here by lucky chance on one of the very few dull days in the glorious summer of 1995. The misty atmosphere was created by oil-based smoke supplied by the property department.

DUCHESS OF YORK

To war take with you my most grievous curse!
My prayers shall on Richmond's party fight.
Bloody you are: bloody will be your end.
Shame serves your life – and will your
death attend!

She has finished cursing.

RICHARD, the resplendent Commander-in-Chief, is ready to leave. Winking at TYRELL who follows, RICHARD pushes past the DUCHESS OF YORK, out into the corridor and off to war. RATCLIFFE marches behind.

Mother and son will not meet again.

99   **EXT. SUBURBAN AERODROME – DUSK**

An Imperial Airways passenger plane, its engines ticking over, is ready to fly across the English Channel to France.

The DUCHESS OF YORK makes her way from her car to the waiting aircraft. QUEEN ELIZABETH and PRINCESS ELIZABETH have come to see her off – both wrapped up against the stiff breeze.

An AIRCRAFTSMAN carries the leather luggage.

'I leave for France.' In the play, it is Queen Margaret who returns to her homeland, France.

scene 100 was filmed at Steamtown Railway Centre at Carnforth in Lancashire. A collection of antique rolling-stock is kept in working order by enthusiasts for steam.

Just across the tracks is the small railway station where David Lean filmed Noel Coward's *Brief Encounter* exactly fifty summers before we too were shooting in Carnforth. RL and I were encouraged by this coincidence, *Brief Encounter* being our favourite British movie – to date!

DUCHESS OF YORK
(above the roar of the engines)
I leave for France. Be not tongue-tied.
You are a dream of what you were, a breath,
A queen in jest. Where is your husband now?
Where is your brother? Where are your two
sons? Wherein joy?
Who sues and kneels and says 'God Save
the Queen'?
Where be the bending peers that flattered you?
Where be the thronging troops that followed
you?

QUEEN ELIZABETH is crying as they kiss goodbye.

The DUCHESS OF YORK is helped onboard the plane by
the AIRCRAFTSMAN.

QUEEN ELIZABETH
(desperately shouting up to the DUCHESS OF
YORK)
O teach me how to curse my enemy!

DUCHESS OF YORK
(shouting back as the steps are moved away)
Forbear to sleep the nights and fast the days.
Think that your babes were sweeter than
they were;
And he that slew them, fouler than he is!

100   **EXT. RAILWAY SIDINGS – DAY**

RICHARD's troops are busily and efficiently preparing for
mobilisation, loading supplies and artillery from the platform
and onto the armoured steam train.

QUEEN ELIZABETH and PRINCESS ELIZABETH.

This was on our first day's shooting – Tuesday, 27 June 1995. It was good to be away from home with a chance to get to know colleagues over a drink or evening meal.

Everyone assumed I must be excited to be filming at last. I only realised that this was unlike any other job when at Steamtown I saw the scale of the enterprise – 200 soldiers from the local barracks, kitted out in black; 20 horses with their grooms; half-a-dozen Alsatians and their handlers; a crew of 50 technicians; Annette Bening; tents, caravans and a catering truck; and a German engine that had been designed to pull Hitler's train across the Third Reich – and all because three years ago I wanted to go on playing Richard III!

Tony Burrough: 'The period carriages are French and English. We invented our own armoured carriages, by painting them to give an armour-plated look. It is full of anachronisms. Train spotters and military buffs will be confused; but the important thing is that we created the right atmosphere to tell the story.'

One of the railway carriages is RICHARD's mobile headquarters.

QUEEN ELIZABETH and PRINCESS ELIZABETH determinedly push their way through the indifferent soldiery, until QUEEN ELIZABETH spies RICHARD and his black-shirted ENTOURAGE striding along the platform to his carriage. She has decided to cause a scene.

> QUEEN ELIZABETH
> (screaming)
> **Tell me, you villain slave, where are
> my children?**

RICHARD stops and turns to her. So do his bodyguards. QUEEN ELIZABETH is unabashed.

> QUEEN ELIZABETH
> (continuing)
> **Where is my brother Rivers and your brother
> Clarence? Where is Lord Hastings?**

> RICHARD
> (beckoning to QUEEN ELIZABETH)
> **Elizabeth!**

RICHARD signals his GUARDS to escort QUEEN ELIZABETH and PRINCESS ELIZABETH, like prisoners, toward the train.

> RICHARD
> (over his shoulder)
> **I must talk a word with you.**

> QUEEN ELIZABETH
> **I have no more sons of the royal blood
> For you to slaughter.**

'You have a daughter called Elizabeth.' Queen Elizabeth's outburst against her enemy has been encouraged by the Duchess of York but the attempt at a direct public humiliation of Richard is undercut by his apparent indifference and the ambiguous threat of this line.

scene 101. The interior scenes of the carriage were filmed on the sound-proofed Stage E at Shepperton Studios. It was a relief to be protected from the noise of traffic which so often held up shooting on the exterior locations to the despair of the sound mixer David Stephenson.

PRINCESS ELIZABETH is detained on the platform and plonked on a bench, between two black-shirted GUARDS.

>RICHARD
>(helping QUEEN ELIZABETH on board)
>**You have a daughter called Elizabeth.**

101 **INT. RICHARD'S CARRIAGE HEADQUARTERS – DAY**

The interior has been stylishly adapted into the main control centre of RICHARD's military headquarters. Veneered panelling and a couple of easy chairs are bolted to the carpeted floor.

CATESBY, TYRELL and other BLACK-SHIRTED SENIOR OFFICERS are working under the shaded overhead lamps that illuminate the table, laid out with maps and battle plans.

>QUEEN ELIZABETH
>**And must she die for this? O, let her live!**

RICHARD offers her a chair. Battle commences.

>RICHARD
>**Her life is safest only in her birth.**

>QUEEN ELIZABETH
>**And only in that safety died her brothers.**

>RICHARD
>**You speak as if that I had slain the Princes.**

QUEEN ELIZABETH

No doubt the murderous knife was dull
   and blunt
Till it was sharpened on your stone-hard heart
To revel in the entrails of my lambs.

RICHARD

Madam, I intend more good to you and yours
Than ever you or yours by me were harmed.

QUEEN ELIZABETH

Tell me what state, what dignity, what honour
Can you bestow on any child of mine?

RICHARD

Even all I have; yes – and myself and all –
Shall I with all, endow a child of yours.

QUEEN ELIZABETH

Be brief, lest that the process of your kindness
Last longer telling than your kindness date.

RICHARD

Then know, that from my soul, I love your
   daughter.
And do intend to make her Queen of England.

QUEEN ELIZABETH is appalled.

QUEEN ELIZABETH

What, *you*?

RICHARD

Even so. What think you of it?

'You mock me, Madam.'

'Say that I did all this for love of her?' He plays the same card of sincere love which worked so well in persuading Lady Anne to marry him: cf. 'it was your heavenly face that set me on' (scene 23). The two wooing scenes mirror each other. The audience will be wondering whether he can pull it off a second time.

QUEEN ELIZABETH
How can you woo her?

RICHARD
That would I learn of you.

QUEEN ELIZABETH
And will you learn of me?

RICHARD
Madam, with all my heart.

QUEEN ELIZABETH
Send to her – by the man who slew her
    brothers –
A pair of bleeding hearts – then will she weep.
Send her a letter of your noble deeds.
Tell her you made away her Uncle Clarence,
Her Uncle Rivers, yes, and for her sake
Made quick conveyance with her good
    Aunt Anne!

RICHARD
You mock me, Madam. This is not the way
To win your daughter.

QUEEN ELIZABETH
There is no other way:
Unless you could put on some other shape.
And not be Richard who has done all this.

RICHARD
Say that I did all this for love of her?

'Men shall deal unadvisedly sometimes.' Richard has the advantage of being in his own controlled environment. Inside his headquarters, his confidence is not fazed by the presence of officers and staff. He always likes an audience.

At the RNT, the whole scene was witnessed by a line of soldiers standing at ease.

'We have many goodly days to see.' Richard makes a bare-faced appeal to Queen Elizabeth's venality by holding out the promise of power and riches. It was a bribe which in the Lady Anne scene was not put into words. Here, it is particularly sickening, in its implication that Queen Elizabeth shares his own immorality. Richard cannot comprehend the depth of her feelings.

'. . . the sweet, silent hours of marriage joys.' This is rich coming from the husband of the ill-fated Lady Anne. I played it with as much conviction as possible, so that Queen Elizabeth and, indeed, the audience might just believe that his conscience is beginning to get the better of him.

QUEEN ELIZABETH

Well then, she cannot choose but hate you.

RICHARD

Look – what is done cannot be now amended.
Men shall deal unadvisedly sometimes.

RICHARD fills a glass of gin, gives it to QUEEN
ELIZABETH and sits opposite her.

RICHARD
(continuing)

If I did take the Kingdom from your sons,
To make amends, I'll give it to your daughter.
Again shall you be mother of a king.
What? We have many goodly days to see.
The liquid drops of tears that you have shed,
Shall come again, transformed to orient pearl.

RICHARD
(continuing)

Go then, my mother. To your daughter go:
Make bold her bashful years, with your
    experience.
Acquaint the Princess
With the sweet, silent hours of marriage joys.
And when these troops of mine have chastised
The petty rebel Richmond and dull-brained
    'Buck-ing-ham',
Bound with triumphant garlands will I come
And lead your daughter to a conqueror's bed.

QUEEN ELIZABETH

What were I best to say?

RICHARD

Say she shall be a high and mighty Queen.

As Queen Elizabeth bitterly responds to Richard's lines by deftly echoing his rhythms and words. He is close to losing his temper. That is why he closes the sliding door between his staff and the increasingly intimate exchange with his most challenging rival.

QUEEN ELIZABETH
To wail the title, as her mother does.

RICHARD
Say – I will love her everlastingly.

QUEEN ELIZABETH
But how long fairly shall her sweet life last?

RICHARD
As long as Heaven and nature lengthen it.

QUEEN ELIZABETH
As long as Hell and Richard like of it.

RICHARD
Your reasons are too shallow and too quick.

QUEEN ELIZABETH
Oh, no. My reasons are too deep and dead.
Too deep and dead, my infants, in their graves.

RICHARD
Harp not on that string, Madam, that is past.

QUEEN ELIZABETH
Harp on it still, shall I, till heartstrings break.

'**I know that Richmond aims to wed Elizabeth.**' The eldest child of the late King Edward would add lustre to Richmond's claim to the throne. Richard exaggerates that the forthcoming war will be fought over the Princess: but his threat is plain. He is determined to hold onto the throne; and the more dangerous Richmond's challenge, the longer war will persist, with all its attendant miseries.

'**Where, in that nest of spicery, they shall breed.**' Richard's sense of the erotic owes more to barrack-room boasting than to the bedroom.

A drama critic of the RNT production, chiding my Richard for not being sexy enough, thought it significant and unfortunate that this line had been cut. Each night onstage, I remembered his comment but did nothing about it until re-instating the line in the screenplay.

RICHARD
(*sotto voce*)
I know that Richmond aims to wed Elizabeth.
In her consists my happiness – and yours.
Without her, follows to myself and you,
Herself, the land and many a Christian soul,
Death, desolation, ruin and decay.
They cannot be avoided – but by this.
Be the attorney of my love to her.
Plead what I will be, not what I have been.

QUEEN ELIZABETH
Shall I be tempted by the Devil thus?

RICHARD
Yes, if the Devil tempt you to do good.

QUEEN ELIZABETH
But you did kill my children.

RICHARD
But in your daughter's womb, I bury them,
Where, in that nest of spicery, they shall breed.

QUEEN ELIZABETH
Shall I go win my daughter to your will?

RICHARD
And be a happy mother by the deed.

QUEEN ELIZABETH
(rising)
Write to me very shortly,
And you shall understand from me her mind.

'Bear her my true love's kiss.' Richard has enjoyed flirting with Queen Elizabeth. This kiss has a double nastiness. As the audience now is accustomed to Kate Steavenson-Payne's innocent prettiness, they can imagine her revulsion were she forced to be intimate with her brothers' killer.

'Lord Stanley, what news?' Stanley is played by Edward Hardwicke. His father, Sir Cedric, as King Edward, was one of the four actor-knights in Olivier's film. Edward was one of Olivier's young recruits to his National Theatre and he does a brilliant impersonation. Previously we had worked only once together, when I directed him as Birdboot in Stoppard's *The Real Inspector Hound* at the Phoenix Theatre in Leicester (1972).

RICHARD
(stopping her)
Bear her my true love's kiss.

RICHARD kisses her full on the mouth. Amazed and revolted, QUEEN ELIZABETH leaves the carriage.

RICHARD
(continuing)
Farewell.

102 **EXT. STATION PLATFORM – DAY**

PRINCESS ELIZABETH rushes away from her GUARDS to QUEEN ELIZABETH's embrace.

RICHARD
(standing at the carriage door, to CAMERA)
Relenting fool! And shallow, changing woman!

He sees LORD STANLEY coming along the platform and pretending to ignore QUEEN ELIZABETH and PRINCESS ELIZABETH, although a look is exchanged. LORD STANLEY makes for RICHARD's carriage.

KING RICHARD
Lord Stanley, what news?

LORD STANLEY
(saluting and nervous)
None good, Your Majesty: nor none so bad –

RICHARD
Hoyday, a riddle! Neither good nor bad?
Once more, what news?

'Richmond is on the seas' was my clue for making him a naval Lieutenant.

'I never was, nor never will be, false.' The upright Stanley, although he never wears the black uniform, is the only person to fool Richard throughout. In history and in the play, the delivery of his troops to Richmond's side was crucial to the defeat of Richard at the Battle of Bosworth. This was perhaps Shakespeare's acknowledgement of one of his patrons, Lord Strange, who was a descendant of the real Lord Stanley.

In the film, it is Stanley's Air Force which is decisive.

LORD STANLEY
Richmond is on the seas.

RICHARD
Then be the seas on him! What does he there?

RICHARD steps down and proceeds along the platform, followed by LORD STANLEY.

LORD STANLEY
Your Majesty, I know not – but by guess.

RICHARD
Well, as you guess?

LORD STANLEY
Stirred up by Buckingham,
He makes for England, here to claim the crown.

RICHARD
Is the throne empty? Is the King dead?
You will revolt and fly to him, I fear.

LORD STANLEY
I never was, nor never will be, false.

RICHARD
(patting his shoulder)
Go then; and muster men.

LORD STANLEY, relieved he has got away with it, salutes and is about to leave. But RICHARD has not finished with him. He stops and directs LORD STANLEY's attention to his son GEORGE, in the friendly control of TYRELL.

Gary Blowfield: Tony Burrough: RL: Ratcliffe: Richard III. After each take there is a chance to review what has just been shot on the video monitor which records in fuzzy black-and-white what the film camera has just seen in colour. Gary Blowfield was in charge.

I always monitored my progress in this way, although it could be unnerving to realise that a performance is basically fixed once the director is satisfied and decides to move on to the next set-up. I found it an invaluable means of checking emotional levels and positions vis-à-vis the camera. 'If it works on the video playback, RL said, it will work twenty-fold at the Odeon Leicester Square.'

'I cry you mercy.' To strike a subordinate is a court-martial offence. It is a shocking incident that reveals Richard's inner lack of confidence. James Dreyfus played the Subaltern. He and I had previously filmed together in *Thin Ice* (1994).

> RICHARD
> (continuing)
> **But leave with us your son, young George.**
> **Stanley, look your heart be firm,**
> **Or else his head's assurance is but frail.**

LORD STANLEY, aghast, retreats along the platform.
TYRELL gently restrains GEORGE from following his
father. He smiles up at his guardian.

As RICHARD is about to mount the train, a young Aryan
SUBALTERN rushes up and hands over his
telegraph message.

> SUBALTERN
> **Your Majesty. The Duke of Buckingham is –**

> RICHARD
> (strikes the SUBALTERN hard on the cheek)
> **Till you bring better news.**

The OFFICERS and SOLDIERS who see this are appalled
that their leader is so out of control.

RATCLIFFE rescues the telegraph message from the ground.

> RATCLIFFE
> (reading)
> **'The Duke of Buckingham is taken prisoner!'**

> RICHARD
> (to SUBALTERN)
> **I cry you mercy.**

RICHARD smartly and graciously embraces the
SUBALTERN and remounts the train, followed by
TYRELL. GEORGE STANLEY is left behind with his
NCO guard.

'Richmond is landed with a mighty power from France – '?

scene 104. This description of mine was based on RL's imagination. Initially it was hoped to film in the Beckton Marshes in east London which Stanley Kubrick used for the battle scenes of *Full Metal Jacket* (1987). But the ground these days is declared unsafe for heavy traffic and so we used the Rye Harbour Nature Reserve, where seabirds are protected on 585 acres of shingle beach, wet gravel pits and farmland.

103 INT. RICHARD'S MILITARY TRAIN – DAY

RICHARD and TYRELL race along the corridor back to carriage headquarters. They are met by a RADIO OPERATOR coming toward them, with another telegraph message.

> SECOND SUBALTERN
> **Richmond is landed with a mighty power**
> **from France –**

> RICHARD
> (back in control)
> **Let's go to meet him! While we reason here,**
> **A royal battle might be won or lost.**

The train sets off.

> RICHARD
> (continuing)
> **Tyrell, give order 'Buck-ing-ham' be brought.**

TYRELL understands the unspoken order.

104 EXT. RIVER THAMES MARSHES – EVENING

Near the wide estuary of a great waterway is a decayed urban landscape, jutting out of waterlogged marshes, where the river has flooded the flat land. Rough roads lead to solitary, imposing electric pylons, whose sagging cables once supplied now abandoned factories. Through the drizzle and low-lying mist, are hulks of listing ships and rusting gasometers. Seabirds scream and crows flap overhead.

From the English Channel, an armada of amphibious landing craft is reaching shore. Military vehicles and tanks churn ashore through the waves. RICHMOND, in naval battlegear, steps on land.

'Fortune and victory be with you, nephew.' In the play, Henry Richmond is son to the Countess of Richmond, through whose blood-line he will claim the throne. On his mother's marriage to Stanley, he becomes Stanley's stepson. It seemed less confusing to call him Stanley's nephew in the film. By appointing him Naval Lieutenant, he could lead a credible military attack from France. Because of his class and his uniform, Richmond is trusted by the Establishment. His insubstantial right to the throne is never questioned: but then there is no other obvious pretender and Richard's universal unpopularity is a huge advantage to any determined opponent.

**'The Queen has heartily consented
That I marry Princess Elizabeth.'**
In the play, this welcome news is delivered to Richmond across the battlelines by Stanley's messenger (4.5).

'I doubt not but his friends will turn to you.' Shakespeare keeps Brackenbury at his post in The Tower. In the film, we needed to show that Richmond had some recognisable supporters. So Brackenbury, guilty about the deaths of the princes in his charge, has decided to take the gamble and join Richmond's invasion.

'He has no friends.' This line is spoken over a distant view of Richard's encampment. The distinctive silhouette of Battersea Power Station was electronically superimposed on the horizon.

LORD STANLEY, in RAF uniform, BRACKENBURY
and the ARCHBISHOP are waiting to welcome the invader.

> LORD STANLEY
> **Fortune and victory be with you, nephew.**

As they all stride forward onto drier ground, LORD
STANLEY hands a telegram for RICHMOND to read.

> RICHMOND
> (as he reads)
> **The Queen has heartily consented**
> **That I marry Princess Elizabeth.**

> ARCHBISHOP
> **England rejoice.**

> LORD STANLEY
> **Prepare your advance early in the morning.**
> **On your side I may not be too forward,**
> **Your cousin George is held in custody.**

> RICHMOND
> **The wretched, bloody and usurping swine!**

> BRACKENBURY
> **I doubt not but his friends will turn to you.**

> LORD STANLEY
> **He has no friends.**

105 **EXT. RICHARD'S ENCAMPMENT – NIGHT**

Some miles inland from RICHMOND's invasion,
RICHARD's forces are encamped around the armoured
train. His black-uniformed TROOPS are sheltered in

This could be Agincourt all over again. Olivier shot his Agincourt in Ireland and his Battle of Bosworth in Spain. I had originally imagined we would fight ours in a rural landscape of mud. RL favoured an urban war-zone and so he set Richard's camp in and around the largest disused building in London, the Battersea Power Station, which for four decades supplied the capital with electricity. Much of the insides have been gutted but the outer structure is preserved by law. Plans for its development as an entertainment centre have faltered for lack of funds. Perhaps the film will encourage Londoners to care more for one of our most distinctive landmarks. It could house an exciting 'Richard III Ride' like at Disneyland or Universal Studios!

'Will not King Richard let me speak with him?' Buckingham dies still not crediting that Richard never needed him as much as he needed Richard.

Tyrell displays a varied repertoire of murder. In the film, he cuts throats, stabs, hangs, smothers and here garrottes. In the play, Richard does not witness this execution, nor even receive confirmation of it, although Buckingham returns as a ghost in Richard's nightmare.

improvised bivouacs and canvas bell-tents, straining at their taut guy-ropes, spattered by the drizzling rain. The marsh grass is turning to mud under the boots of troops, the wheels of armoured vehicles and the horses' hooves.

From far and near, men call to each other, horses whinny, dogs bark, engines rev and a bugle sounds. This could be Agincourt all over again – or the Crimea or the Somme.

106 INT. CANVAS-ROOFED ARMY TRUCK – NIGHT

TYRELL at work, in the back of the truck parked in the mud.

BUCKINGHAM is on his knees, trussed up. He has been tortured. His clothes are torn, his body beaten and bruised.

TYRELL moves in to garrotte BUCKINGHAM.

> BUCKINGHAM
> **Will not King Richard let me speak with him?**

> TYRELL
> **No, my good Lord.**

> BUCKINGHAM
> **Made I him King for this?**

As TYRELL's wire tightens round BUCKINGHAM's neck we see familiar eyes reflected in the driving-mirror. RICHARD is sitting unobserved in the passenger seat. He watches as BUCKINGHAM's life is choked from him.

> RICHARD (V.O.)
> **Tyrell, why look you so sad?**

scene 107. In the play, Richard twice asks for wine within eight lines, a clear indication that he is drinking too much as he prepares his battle plans. Earlier he has struck the Subaltern. No wonder Ratcliffe and Tyrell look apprehensive.

107   INT. RICHARD'S CARRIAGE – NIGHT

A bed has been pulled down from the wall. Otherwise, it's still the command centre as before.

RICHARD is seated, a little the worse for drink.

TYRELL and RATCLIFFE are standing with him – they are worried. CATESBY too.

> TYRELL
> **My heart is ten times lighter than my looks.**

> RICHARD
> (grinning)
> **What is it o'clock?**

> RATCLIFFE
> **It's supper-time, Your Majesty.**

> RICHARD
> (emptying his glass and holding it out)
> **I will not sup tonight.**
> **What is the number of the traitors?**

> RATCLIFFE
> (filling RICHARD's glass)
> **Six or seven thousand, Your Majesty.**

> RICHARD
> **Why, our battalions treble that account.**
> **Besides, the King's name is a tower of strength,**

> (dismissing TYRELL)
> **Stir with the lark tomorrow, gentle Tyrell.**

'lest his son George . . .' Stanley's son survives in the play 'safe in Leicester town'. In the film, he can be glimpsed sheltering from the confusion of battle in scene 121.

'I will.' In the play, Catesby is loyal to Richard to the end, acting as an adjutant. In the film, he sees that Richard's star is falling. Tim McInnerny chose this moment to indicate that Catesby was leaving to consider his own future. Richard does not notice.

Catesby's last lines from the play are shared by Tyrell and Ratcliffe in scene 123.

> TYRELL
> **Your Majesty.**

TYRELL salutes and leaves.

> RICHARD
> (shouting as if CATESBY were outside)
> **Catesby!**

> CATESBY
> (quietly at RICHARD's side)
> **Your Majesty?**

> RICHARD
> **Send to Lord Stanley. Bid him bring his force**
> **Before sun-rising, lest his son George fall**
> **Into the blind cave of eternal night**
> **Leave me.**

> CATESBY
> **I will.**

CATESBY leaves with a nod to RATCLIFFE, who salutes and turns to go. He turns to see RICHARD trying to massage the pain out of his crippled arm. RICHARD looks up.

> RICHARD
> (continuing; sternly)
> **Leave me, I say.**

RATCLIFFE, worried, leaves. RICHARD drinks and closes his eyes.

scene 108. In the play, Queen Elizabeth vanishes after her confrontation with Richard. RL and I wanted to complete her story with one last glimpse of her revenge. She is the principal survivor in the film.

'O Lord, let Richmond and Elizabeth . . .' The marriage of Richmond and Elizabeth is not in the play although their union is announced in Richmond's closing speech (5.5) which here provides the Archbishop's lines.

108 INT. RICHMOND'S HEADQUARTERS – NIGHT

RICHMOND kneels with PRINCESS ELIZABETH in
front of a makeshift altar, presided over by the
ARCHBISHOP. Holy Communion has just been
completed. QUEEN ELIZABETH looks on, satisfied.

> ARCHBISHOP
> (praying)
> **O Lord, let Richmond and Elizabeth**
> **By Your fair ordinance be joined together,**
> **And let their heirs – God, if Thy will be so –**
> **Enrich the time to come with smooth-faced**
> ** peace.**

RICHMOND gently kisses his bride-to-be and then closes
his eyes.

> RICHMOND
> **O Thou, whose captain I account myself,**
> **Look on my forces with a gracious eye.**
> **Put in their hands Thy bruising arms of wrath,**
> **That we may praise Thee in Thy victory.**
> **Sleeping and waking, O, defend me still.**

109 INT. RICHARD'S CARRIAGE – NIGHT

RICHARD lies restless in his bed. He turns and flinches in
his sleep. His eyes flicker and dart under the closed lids.

110 INT. RICHARD'S NIGHTMARE OF DESPAIR

The deaths of RICHARD's murdered victims are re-enacted
with the CAMERA as the victims' eyes. RICHARD sees
what they saw at the moment of their deaths.

scenes 111-15: Holinshed refers to a 'dreadful and terrible dream which stuffed his head and troubled his mind'. An earlier play, *The True Tragedy of Richard III* (1594), which Shakespeare could have seen, has the hero terrorised by 'my wounded conscience'. In his own play, the young Shakespeare dares to present the dream onstage and then with double daring to have it shared between Richard and Richmond. At the RNT, the murdered figures moved between the two sleeping commanders. Onscreen, such a dream could be easily effective. However, our emphasis is laid on Richard's waking speech, his last to camera.

scene 116. In the theatre, this speech can get lost within the turbulent preparations for battle which are more prolonged than in the film. Cinematic close-up gives the speech its proper importance.

'Richard loves Richard; that is, I am I.' In a remarkable speech, this is the most remarkable line. Throughout, much of the 'full text' uses rhetorical devices of regular rhythm, rhymes, repetitions and alliteration. Here Shakespeare's words are as modern and as bleak as Samuel Beckett's. Apart from 'loves' and the simple monosyllables 'that', 'is' and 'am', the rest is all 'Richard' by name or pronoun. The second 'I' is stressed by its rhyme with 'by'. The line explains everything. Unloved from birth by even his mother, he could only make sense of life by loving himself and hating the rest of the world. Is this tragic? Certainly he has visited tragedy on his victims and on their survivors. His newfound conscience underlines a tragic sense of waste.

111   CLARENCE is pushed under his bath water and a rush of
      blood billows away from CAMERA.

112   RIVERS sees his chest pierced by his assailant's blade.

113   HASTINGS sees the hangman's noose placed over his head.

114   The screen is covered by the red silk, as PRINCE JAMES
      is smothered.

115   BUCKINGHAM struggles as the garrotting-wire passes
      before his eyes and he sees RICHARD in the
      driving-mirror.

116   **INT. RICHARD'S CARRIAGE – NIGHT**

      RICHARD tries to scream in his agony of guilt but cannot,
      until he wakes up. He is sweating with fear.

                    RICHARD
          I did but dream! O, coward conscience.
          What do I fear? Myself? There's none else by –
          Richard loves Richard; that is, I am I.
      He looks nervously around at his empty carriage.

'Oh Ratcliffe.' This was my first opportunity to act with Bill Paterson, although I had worked with his wife Hildegarde Beckler when she designed *King Lear*, the production which partnered *Richard III* at the RNT. He appeared in RL's *The Vanishing Army*, one of his many films. I am always amazed at the masterly naturalism of Bill's performances on stage, television and film. He usually insists on acting with his native Scottish accent. Even so, he was unforgettable as Harry The Horse in Richard Eyre's *Guys and Dolls* at the RNT (1982).

RICHARD
(continuing)
Is there a murderer here? No. Yes – I am.
I love myself. But why? For any good
That I myself have done unto myself?
O no. Alas, I rather hate myself,
For hateful deeds committed by myself.
I am a villain. Yet I lie – I am not.
Fool, of yourself speak well.
Fool, do not flatter.
My conscience has a thousand, several tongues
Thronged to the bar, crying all: 'Guilty! Guilty!'
I shall despair. There is no creature loves me:
And if I die, no soul will pity me.

RATCLIFFE enters, disturbed by RICHARD's outcry.

RATCLIFFE
(quietly)
Your Majesty . . .

RICHARD jumps at his voice.

RICHARD
Oh Ratcliffe.
Will all our friends prove true?

RATCLIFFE
No doubt, Your Majesty.

RICHARD
Ratcliffe, I fear . . . I fear.

RATCLIFFE
(daring to comfort him)
No, Your Majesty: be not afraid of shadows.

RICHARD looks up into the reliable face of his faithful batman and smiles. RICHARD's himself again.

117 EXT. RICHMOND'S ARMY ENCAMPMENT – MARSHES – DAWN

A vale of mist drifts through the tented city. Trucks and tanks roar into life as an orange sun rises over the bleak and desolate shore. The army is on the move.

118 INT. RICHMOND'S HEADQUARTERS – MARSHES – DAWN

PRINCESS ELIZABETH watches over the sleeping RICHMOND.

He stirs as she gently strokes his face.

> PRINCESS ELIZABETH
> **How have you slept, my Lord?**

> RICHMOND
> (smiling)
> **The sweetest sleep, the fairest-boding dreams**
> **That ever entered in a drowsy head.**

119 EXT. RICHARD'S ENCAMPMENT – DAWN

A steady drizzle. Tanks and armour churn through the cloying mud. Men shout above the engines' roar. Like ants, each with his purpose, RICHARD's forces prepare for battle.

scene 120. I was nervous about being close to the controlled explosion within the carriage, particularly when I saw an ambulance waiting outside the studio. Jim Dowdall, who brilliantly and safely co-ordinated all the stunts, reassured me that this precaution was quite usual – as was my reaction to it. The pyrotechnics were at the far end of the carriage, away from Bill Paterson and me. We had our backs to the shattered, imitation glass in the foreground and only had to make sure we fell safely to the floor as the carriage was rocked sharply to one side.

120 INT. RICHARD'S CARRIAGE – DAWN

> RICHARD
> **Conscience is but a word that cowards use.**
> **Remember whom you are to cope withall,**
> **A sort of vagabonds, rascals and runaways.**
> **And who does lead them but a paltry fellow:**
> **A milksop!**
> **If we be conquered, let men conquer us!**
> **Let's whip these peasants over the seas again.**
> **Shall these enjoy our lands? Lie with our wives?**
> **Ravish our daughters?**

RICHARD turns to TYRELL, as he enters the carriage, anxious for his news.

> RICHARD
> (continuing)
> **What says Lord Stanley? Will he bring his force?**

> TYRELL
> **My Lord, he has refused to come to you.**

> RICHARD
> **Off with his son George's head!**

Before TYRELL or RATCLIFFE can reply or move, the approaching drone of aircraft overhead signals that LORD STANLEY's forces have arrived – to bomb the hell out of RICHARD and his troops. An almighty explosion shatters the end of the carriage. The battle has begun.

121 EXT. RICHARD'S ENCAMPMENT – DAY

Chaos. The surprise attack of STANLEY's bombers has wreaked havoc. Through the murk of smoke and flame, in and around the huge, empty buildings, Richard's

RICHARD mans a machine-gun . . . Each military vehicle was painted with a number and 'R III'.

'A horse! A horse! My kingdom for a horse!' Onstage I fought the battle in full medieval armour, despite the 30s setting. In my first draft of the screenplay I wrote:

> RICHARD limps out of the smoke, a banner in his hand, from helmet to toe in silver armour. A heavenly romantic fanfare, as the sounds of battle fade at this vision of chivalry.

>

> RICHARD
> **A horse! A horse! My kingdom for a horse!**
>

> RICHMOND, a 20th-century commando takes aim. His bullet explodes on RICHARD's head. RICHARD collapses in the mud and dies instantly, ingloriously. RICHMOND's boot turns RICHARD over, now in modern black.

This might just have worked had my description of the battle been more specific:

> Through the murk of mist and smoke, it is impossible to tell the progress of the battle.

To be sure, Shakespeare is not much more helpful:

> Alarum: excursions. Forces fighting. Alarum. Enter Richard with Richmond; they fight; Richard is slain.

I left it to RL to invent the progression of the battle in its modern urban setting. His instructions were hand-drawn on a 'story-board', like a kid's comic, so we could all understand each detail between Richard's last line in the play and his last line in the film.

SOLDIERS are in confusion. Everything dreadful about war is felt in appalling sights and sounds.

Screams of panic, fear and death.

122 **EXT. MARSH LAND – DAY**

Steadily, RICHMOND and his ARMOURED TROOPS proceed across the difficult ground toward RICHARD's forces. Tanks, artillery, armoured cars, even horses – anything to convey the invasion relentlessly onward.

123 **EXT. RICHARD'S HEADQUARTERS – DAY**

Many of the buildings and the armoured train are ablaze from the bombing. The sky is black with acrid smoke.

RICHARD is magnificent as he tries to rally his troops. When there is a second devastating attack from the air, RICHARD mans a machine-gun and fires at the planes.

He jumps into an armoured vehicle, which RATCLIFFE revs into life. But its heavy wheels churn the rain-soaked mud and sink lower into it. There is no way out.

>RICHARD
>**A horse! A horse! My kingdom for a horse!**

RATCLIFFE still revs the engine, as he sees TYRELL plodding towards RICHARD's vehicle.

>RATCLIFFE
>**Rescue! James Tyrell, rescue! Rescue!**

>TYRELL
>(opening the vehicle's door)
>**Escape, Your Majesty! I'll help you to a horse!**

'Escape? Slave!' cf. the anonymous *The True Tragedy of Richard III* (1594):

> King: A horse, a horse, a fresh horse.
> Page: Ah fly my lord and save your life.
> King: Fly villain? Look I as though I would fly? No!

Onstage, at the suggestion that Richard should withdraw, I hit out at the speaker. Richard has nothing left but his bravery. Catesby has gone, Ratcliffe is dying and now the other faithful follower, the reliable Tyrell, suggests deserting the battle. It is time for Richard to be entirely on his own.

scene 124. From here to the end very little is what it seems to be. With the exception of the distant figure limping along the uppermost girder (my double, Dave Cronnelly) and the final fall, the rest is me but rarely at the apparent distance from terra firma.

RICHARD
Escape? Slave!

RICHARD levels his revolver and fires point blank into TYRELL'S face.

Still the wheels sink into the mud.

As RICHARD clambers down, RICHMOND's troops are within sight.

A quick, final decision. RICHARD will defy the inevitable. He races away from RATCLIFFE, through explosions and enemy fire, toward the vast shell of a burning bombed-out building. Behind we see RATCLIFFE and the armoured vehicle blown high into the air.

RICHMOND's own command vehicle is pushing through the smoke, like a hunter.

124 **INT. BOMBED-OUT BUILDING – DAY**

Inside the shell of a massive abandoned factory, the devastating bombing has set ruptured fuel tanks alight. Thick smoke mingles with billowing red clouds of burning oil.

RICHARD stumbles through the tangle of girders and smashed concrete, looking for a route up to some vantage point, to fire on RICHMOND. He looks up at the sagging girders on which he could climb to what remains of the roof.

125 **EXT. BOMBED-OUT BUILDING – DAY**

RICHMOND's troops are arriving thick and fast and slaughtering any remaining defenders in hand-to-hand combat.

RICHMOND and his PLATOON carefully enter the building, looking for RICHARD.

'Let's to it pell-mell,
If not to Heaven, then hand-in-hand to Hell!'
    This couplet is from Richard's rallying speech to his officers before the battle (5.3). In the play, Richard's final line is a repetition of 'A horse! A horse! My kingdom for a horse!'

It was RL's plausible suggestion that Richard should commit suicide – Richmond's bullet is superfluous as its target falls to his certain hellish death in the flames below.
    As Richmond then usurps Richard's privilege and smiles into the camera, are we to be charmed and relieved that he is ready to rule? It is unimaginable that King Richmond might copy Richard's unique wickedness. Yet, Richmond's grin is unsettling. He has more conviction than Fortinbras, Malcolm, Edgar, who, exhausted, pick up the pieces elsewhere in Shakespeare. The future is a question mark. I don't suppose there was much dancing in the streets of Berlin on VE Day.

When RL invited me to see the first rough-cut of *Richard III* at the studios of Interact in west London a month after shooting, I relished the double irony of the Al Jolson song which he had overlaid on the final frames of his film. Richmond and Richard, simultaneously feel, in the moment when their fates collide, that they are sitting on top of the world.

126 INT. BOMBED-OUT BUILDING – DAY

RICHARD is clambering up the steel girders.
RICHMOND spies him and, covered by his PLATOON,
he too starts climbing.

RICHMOND is not disabled. He is younger than
RICHARD and is soon advancing on him. Neither soldier
can get a clear sighting of the other.

One hundred feet up, RICHARD drags himself onto a
narrow ledge. As he does so his machine pistol slips from his
grasp, lost into the flame and smoke below.

RICHARD realises that there is no possible way further up –
or below him. RICHMOND climbs nearer.

RICHMOND pulls himself level with RICHARD. He
prepares to fire at the sitting target, the throne only a
bullet away.

> RICHARD
> (smilingly challenging at RICHMOND)
> **Let's to it pell-mell,**
> **If not to Heaven, then hand-in-hand to Hell!**

RICHARD steps calmly out into space. At exactly the same
moment RICHMOND pulls the trigger.

RICHARD's body falls and spins in slow motion toward the
burning hell below.

TITLES OVER: Images of RICHARD's body as it falls
through the hell of smoke and flames

"What the hell do you think
you're doing to my play?"

CAST
(in order of appearance)

Prince Edward	Christopher Bowen
King Henry	Edward Jewesbury
Richard III	Ian McKellen
Ratcliffe	Bill Paterson
Queen Elizabeth	Annette Bening
Young Prince	Matthew Groom
King Edward	John Wood
Clarence	Nigel Hawthorne
Duchess of York	Maggie Smith
Princess Elizabeth	Kate Steavenson-Payne
Rivers	Robert Downey Jr
Air Hostess	Tres Hanley
Catesby	Tim McInnerny
Ballroom Singer	Stacey Kent
Hastings	Jim Carter
Archbishop	Roger Hammond
Lord Mayor	Dennis Lill
Buckingham	Jim Broadbent
Stanley	Edward Hardwicke
George Stanley	Ryan Gilmore
Richmond	Dominic West
Brackenbury	Donald Sumpter
Lady Anne	Kristin Scott Thomas
Tyrell	Adrian Dunbar
Jailer	Andy Rashleigh
Prince of Wales	Marco Williamson
City Gentleman	Bruce Purchase
1st Subaltern	James Dreyfus
2nd Subaltern	David Antrobus

CREDITS

Mayfair Entertainment International presents
With the participation of British Screen
A Bayly/Paré Production
In association with United Artists Pictures
Developed in association with First Look Pictures

RICHARD III

Associate Producers	Mary Richards and Michele Tandy
Line Producer	David Lascelles
Casting Director	Irene Lamb
Costume Designer	Shuna Harwood
Editor	Paul Green
Production Designer	Tony Burrough
Director of Photography	Peter Biziou BSc
Music	Trevor Jones
Executive Producer	Ellen Dinerman Little
	Ian McKellen
	Joe Simon
	Maria Apodiacos
Producers	Lisa Katselas Paré
	Stephen Bayly
Director	Richard Loncraine

Stunt Co-ordinator
Jim Dowdall

Horsemaster	Steve Dent
Stuntmen	Leo Sheward
	Nick Hobbs
	Jonathan Cohen

	Steve Street
	Paul Heaseman
	Julian Spencer
	Mark Henson
	Steve Griffin
	Mark Lisbon
	Gary Powell
Stunt Fall Performed By	Dave Cronnelly

Developed in Association with
Red Rooster Pictures

Production Executive
Grainne Marmion

Production Co-Ordinator	Erica Bensly
Assistant Production Co-Ordinator	Simon Fraser
Production Assistant	Caroline Moore
Producer's Assistant	Anushka Athaide
Assistant to Ian McKellen	Mig Kimpton
Post-Production Assistant	Sandra Frieze
Location Manager	Charles Hubbard
Co-Location Manager	Adam Richards
Unit Manager	Ken Holt
1st Assistant Director	Ken Tuohy
2nd Assistant Directors	Mark Layton
	Neil Tuohy
	Todd Austin
Floor Runner	Charlie Somers
Script Supervisor	Maria Apodiacos
Casting Consultant USA	Lisa Beach
Camera Operator	Peter Taylor
Focus Puller	Robert Binnall
Clapper Loader	Craig Bloor
Key Grip	Kenny Atherfold
Camera Trainee	Rosalyn Ellis

Crane Operator	Colin Hazell
Video Operator	Gary Blowfield
Video Assistant	Francoise Higson
2nd Camera Operator	John Palmer
2nd Camera Focus Puller	Mark Moriarty
2nd Camera Clapper Loader	Clive Prior
2nd Camera Grip	Joe Felix
Sound Recordist	David Stephenson
Sound Maintenance	Gerry Bates
Sound Trainee	John Lewis
Playback Operator	Mike Harris

Prosthetics and Ian McKellen's Make-up Designed by
Daniel Parker
of Animated Extras

Chief Make-up Artist	Pat Hay
Make-up Artists	Sally Evans
	Kathy Ducker
Chief Hairdresser	Stephen Rose
Hairdresser	Liz Michie
Wardrobe Supervisor	Alan Flyng
Wardrobe Assistants	Sheila Cullen
	Martin 'Elvis' Davis
	Victoria Harwood
Assistant Accountants	Sarah Booth
	Rajeshree Patel
Post-Production Accountant	Andy Hennigan
Art Directors	Choi Ho Man
	Richard Bridgland
Production Buyer	Dominic Smithers
Assistant Art Directors	Sarah Jane Cornish
	Jon Billington

Art Department Assistant	Rebecca Loncraine
Storyboard Artists	John Greaves
	Douglas Ingram
Property Master	Ty Teiger
Property Storeman	Paul Cheesman
Chargehand Dressing Propman	Martin Kingsley
Dressing Propmen	Keith Pitt
	Peter Watson
Chargehand Standby Propman	Jonathan Hurst
Standby Propman	Nick Turnbull
Standby Carpenter	Tommy Westbrook
Standby Rigger	Con Murphy
Standby Painter	Ken Hawkey
Standby Stagehand	Brian Mitchell
Construction Manager	John Godfrey
Assistant Construction Manager	Brian Neighbour
Carpenters	Michael Davis
	Charles Hammett
	David Lowen
	Peter Murray
	Michael Bates
	Steve Furneaux
	Adam Kyriakou
	Tony Musk
	Harry Portlock
	Tony Snook
Supervising Painter	Steve Williamson
Painters	Nick Wood
	Butch Roper
	Dave Thompson
	Arthur Healey
	Alan Tagg
Chargehand Rigger	Frankie Webster

Riggers	Sid Skinner
	Danny Webster
Electrical Riggers	Tim Murphy
	Alan Williams
Chargehand Stagehand	Keith Muir
Stagehands	Steve Malin
	Gary Dyer
	Kevin Day
Chief Lighting Technician	Peter Bloor
Asst Chief Lighting Technician	Ray Meehan
Best Boy	David Ridout
Lighting Technicians	Mark (Rocky) Evans
	Ronnie Phillips
	Sam Bloor
Generator Operator	Alan Grosch
Lighting Rigging Crew	Darren Gatrell
	John Barry
	Ron Lyons
	Dean Wilkenson

Special Effects Supervisor
John Evans

Senior Special Effects Technicians	Barry Whitrod
	Peter Skehan
	Robert Nugent
Special Effects Technicians	Peter Dimmer
	Dave Watkins
	Matthew Horton
	Phil Clark
Special Effects Assistants	John Coyle
	James Skipsey
	David Eves
Post-Production Supervisor	Mike Nunn
1st Assistant Editor/ADR Editor	Elaine 'Chucks' Thomas
2nd Assistant Editor	James Carew

Sound Editor	Philip Bothamley
Dialogue Editor	William Parnell
Foley Editor	Rocky Phelan
Assistant Foley Editor	David Brady
Dubbing Mixers	Aad Wirtz
	Lee Taylor
Music Orchestrations	Trevor Jones
	Julian Kershaw
	Geoff Alexander
Songs Arranged by	Trevor Jones
	Julian Kershaw
	Geoff Alexander
	Colin Good
Music Recorded and Mixed by	Kirsty Whalley
	Paul Golding
Assistant Engineers	Toby Wood
	James Manning
	Eric Jordan
Orchestra Recorded and Mixed at	CTS Studios, London
Synthesizers Recorded at	CMMP Studio, London
Copyist	Tony Stanton
Music Co-Ordinator for CMMP	Victoria Seale
Orchestral Contractor	Isobel Griffiths
Leader	Gavin Wright
Sax and Flute Solo	Phil Todd
Executive Producer (Music)	Mike Batt

Digital Effects Director
Jon Bunker

Digital Effects by	Digital Film at the Moving Picture Company
Visual Effects Producers	Matthew Holben
	Arthur Windus

Compositors	Richard Bain
	Charlie Noble
	Mark Stannard
Film Recording	Frazer Churchill
Stills Photographer	Alex Bailey
Unit Publicists	Charles McDonald
	Patricia Johnson
	McDonald Rutter Ltd.
Dialogue Coach	Andrew Jack
Unit Nurse	Rosie Bedford-Stradling
Health and Safety	Brian Shemmings
Ambulance Services Supplied by	Capital Ambulance & Paramedic Service
Military Adviser	Joceyln Skottowe
Extras Casting by	Ray Knight
Military Extras Supplied by	Ken Whitfield
Stand-Ins	Steve Morphew
	Emma Stokes
Aviation Consultants	Francois Prins
	Etienne Bol
Unit Drivers	Terry Reece
	Gerry Floyd
	Terry English
	Mike Smith
Unit Cars Supplied by	Focus Transport
Facility Vehicles	D & D International Location Facilities
	Roadrunner Film Services
Drivers	Mike Harris
	Scott Henley
	Bob Valles
	John Ott

Bert Griffin
Tony Foster
Albert Smith
Barry Stone
Dennis Swan
Bob Dean
Charlie Thomas
Mike Bartlett

Catering Supplied by   Set Meals

Original Processing & Prints by   Technicolor
Rushes Grader   Huw Phillips
Grader   Peter Hunt

Originated on
Eastman Colour Film from
Kodak

Camera Equipment Supplied by   J. D. & C. Limited
Grip Equipment/Cranes Supplied by Grip House Limited
Lighting Equipment Supplied by   Lee Lighting Limited
Editing and Sound Mixing Facilities Interact Sound Limited

Armourers/Guns Supplied by   Bapty's Limited
Costumes Supplied by   Angels & Bermans Limited

Legal Services   Robert Storer of
                                 Harbottle & Lewis
Insurance   Rollins Hudig Hall Limited
Completion Bond   International Film Guarantors, Inc.
Titles by   General Screen Enterprises
Dolby Consultant   John Iles
OTS Consultant   John Taylor

The Producers would like to thank:

Shell UK for the use of Shell-Mex House
Brown & Mason Limited
Nuclear Electric plc
Steamtown Railway Centre, Carnforth
London Borough of Camden
Sammy's
Major B. Graham &
The Royal Army Medical Corps/Fulwood
Roomloc International
John Buckley   Malcolm Burgess   Bob Crowdey   Pene Delmage
Joe Dunton   John Ensby   Paul Olliver   Ron Pearce

Special Thanks to:
Tony Athaide   Tasso and Jane Katselas
and

Graham Bradstreet	David Elstein
Michael Foster	Roger Holmes
Premila Hoon	Linda James
Robbie Little	Anday McCarron
James Middleton	Nigel Palmer
Simon Perry Kate Wilson	Ann Wingate

'Come Be My Love'
Words by Christopher Marlowe
Performed by Stacey Kent and the Vile Bodies
Composed by Trevor Jones
Arranged by Colin Good
Published by EMI Music Publishing Ltd.

'I'm Sitting on Top of the World'
Performed by Al Jolson
Composed by Ray Henderson, Joe Young and Sam Lewis
Published by EMI United Partnership Ltd.
Redwood Music Corp.
Anglo-Pic Music Co. Ltd.
EMI Catalog Partnership/EMI Feist Catalog Inc.
Ray Henderson Music Corp.